Beyond Juggling

Beyond Juggling

REBALANCING YOUR BUSY LIFE

Kurt Sandholtz
Brooklyn Derr
Kathy Buckner
Dawn Carlson

BK

BERRETT-KOEHLER PUBLISHERS, INC.
San Francisco

Berrett-Koehler Publishers, Inc.
235 Montgomery Street, Suite 650
San Francisco, CA 94104-2916
Tel: (415) 288-0260   Fax: (415) 362-2512   www.bkconnection.com

ORDERING INFORMATION

Quantity sales. Special discounts are available on quantity purchases by corporations, associations, and others. For details, contact the "Special Sales Department" at the Berrett-Koehler address above.

Individual sales. Berrett-Koehler publications are available through most bookstores. They can also be ordered direct from Berrett-Koehler: Tel: (800) 929-2929; Fax: (802) 864-7626; www.bkconnection.com

Orders for college textbook/course adoption use. Please contact Berrett-Koehler: Tel: (800) 929-2929; Fax: (802) 864-7626.

Orders by U.S. trade bookstores and wholesalers. Please contact Publishers Group West, 1700 Fourth Street, Berkeley, CA 94710. Tel: (510) 528-1444; Fax: (510) 528-3444.

Berrett-Koehler and the BK logo are registered trademarks of Berrett-Koehler Publishers, Inc.

Printed in the United States of America

Berrett-Koehler books are printed on long-lasting acid-free paper. When it is available, we choose paper that has been manufactured by environmentally responsible processes. These may include using trees grown in sustainable forests, incorporating recycled paper, minimizing chlorine in bleaching, or recycling the energy produced at the paper mill.

Library of Congress Cataloging-in-Publication Data
Beyond juggling : rebalancing your busy life / Kurt Sandholtz . . . [et al.].
      p. cm.
Includes bibliographical references and index.
  ISBN 1-57675-202-X
  ISBN 1-57675-130-9 (pbk.)
  1. Quality of life. 2. Time management. I. Sandholtz, Kurt, 1959–
BF637.C5 .B466 2002
640'.43—dc21   2002018373

Copyediting and proofreading by PeopleSpeak.
Book design and composition by Beverly Butterfield, Girl of the West Productions.

FIRST EDITION
07   06   05   04   03   02   10 9 8 7 6 5 4 3 2 1

For our mothers,

who taught us to love

the abundance of life.

CONTENTS

PREFACE

THANKSGIVING DAY: A time to pause and reflect on our bounteous blessings; a holiday dedicated to family, friends, food, and football; a brief break that offers few hours of rest and relaxation—and we, the authors of this book, are chained to our computers working on a manuscript about rebalancing our out-of-control lives. An irony this rich doesn't come along all that often. It ought to be savored, along with the feast our families are about to enjoy without us. But we're at present a bit preoccupied.

Sometimes, the role of the author is that of objective reporter or dispassionate analyst. This is not one of those times. In the struggle for a more satisfying, less hectic daily existence, we're full-fledged combatants. Kurt wonders how to raise six children, coach soccer, fulfill a meaningful leadership role at church, help out at home so that his wife can train for a 10K, and survive a high-travel job. Brooklyn faces the pressures of serving on the faculties at two business schools (one in France), keeping up with his academic discipline and maintaining his global industry contacts, while supporting his wife's career and keeping in touch with his children, grandchildren, and garden. For Kathy, the challenge is to take her turn hosting the weekly family dinner, spend time with her aging parents, deal with the premature loss of a beloved sister, help her nephew with his math, and still bring in $1 million worth of business. Dawn has six-month-old twins—need we say more?—in addition to a two-year-old (not yet potty trained), and she recently switched to a new university, where she's now under the microscope of tenure review, as is her husband.

We're not fishing for sympathy here, just establishing our credentials. Beneath this intense personal interest in work-life balance, however, lie equally strong professional motivations. For years, Brooklyn has been fascinated by the forces that shape career decisions, having written numerous articles and a previous book on the subject. Dawn has dedicated much of her research to the dynamics of work-family conflict. Kathy and Kurt, who've taught career planning seminars inside large corporations for ten years, have counseled hundreds of people who identify work-life balance as one of their dominant career goals but see little hope of achieving it.

The ideas in this book began to take shape as we interviewed many of these balance seekers, documenting the methods they employ in their quest. Most were jugglers, trying to do it all through sheer determination, optimal time management, and lots of coffee— and feeling frustrated and overwhelmed in the process. In addition, much of the work-life literature we reviewed (both popular and scholarly) earnestly admired the problem but offered few practical solutions for individuals. We kept digging, believing there had to be techniques beyond juggling for staying committed to one's profession without sacrificing life outside of work.

This book is about what we found—and didn't find. For example, the pages that follow contain no magic formula for work-life balance. Instead, we present a number of workable alternatives to juggling and describe a way to rebalance your on- and off-the-job commitments. For most people, the process involves a series of small adjustments based on conscious trade-offs and leads to a more balanced (or, at least, less unbalanced) life. Stretched as we are, we've applied a number of these techniques ourselves. The results? Not exactly nirvana, but we saw a noticeable, incremental improvement.

A brief word about the nature of balance: It's anything but a one-size-fits-all phenomenon. What feels fast-paced but fun to one person may seem frantic to another. In general, though, we see three essential components to balance: meaningful work, satisfying relationships, and rejuvenating self-care. Admittedly, the self-care part is a sprawling collection of everything from spirituality to recreation. For the sake of simplicity, the book often refers to balance as a dichotomy: work-life (or work-nonwork). Such references are for convenience only. We are not suggesting that "work" isn't part of "life" or that relationships and hobbies never require "work." Please interpret the term "work-life balance" as shorthand for "balance between paid work and the rest of life."

Attitudes toward work and life have changed dramatically since we started this project two years ago. Then, a booming economy and stock market gave people greater freedom of choice in their careers. Balance seemed like a higher-order need that could be indulged, even demanded of prospective employers. As we prepare to send this book to press, the world is in a recession and our nation is at war. New layoffs are announced almost daily. People are feeling less secure. Work-life balance can appear temporarily out of reach, even off the radar screen. Yet, paradoxically, times of crisis often prompt people to reexamine their priorities—and when that happens, balance often tops the list.

In short, the perfect moment for rebalancing one's life never arrives because it never departs. It's always here, right now, in the present—even on Thanksgiving Day, when we're grinding away to meet a deadline. Perhaps it's time to shut down the computer and join our families in a celebration of our abundant (a more flattering word than out-of-control) lives.

Kurt Sandholtz
Brooklyn Derr
Kathy Buckner
Dawn Carlson

ACKNOWLEDGMENTS

IN THE TIME since we began writing this book, a great many people have helped us keep it moving forward. We are grateful to all of them, though we know we'll forget some. We beg your forgiveness if we have inadvertently left you off the list here.

First, each of us needs to thank our families, who not only were willing to put up with our absence for the past year but gave unfailing support for what turned out to be a longer effort than anticipated. We assured them we were alternating (see chapter 3), and that we would make it up to them during a less hectic time. (Now they have it in writing.)

Next, each author wishes to thank his or her coauthors. Despite warnings that we shouldn't write a book together if we wanted to remain friends, we did it anyway. And we're still friends. In fact, the hours we spent together, agonizing over these ideas, were actually fun—a prime example of bundling (see chapter 5).

A number of people pitched in to gather and interpret data, either by conducting interviews or deepening the literature review. Their perspectives and insights contributed enormously to the book's research base. These people include Sharon Duguid, Rebecca Miles, Diana Aron Pfaender, Nathalie Tessier, and Jennifer Lindsey. Zach Derr painstakingly documented all of the citations. Michelle

Harrison gave crucial last-minute assistance on the Balance Strategies Profile (see chapter 9) and reviewed the drafts of the final chapters.

Then there were those whose talents for editing and writing have greatly refined the book's message. First came Lavina Fielding Andersen, with the task of crafting a solid initial draft from Brooklyn's rough notes. Steve Piersanti acted not just as our publisher but as a sort of literary architect, relentlessly pushing us to focus on the "big idea." Louisa Dalton brought her witty and economical style to many of the chapters, and Jerie Jacobs's critical eye helped sharpen the book's opening pages.

Dave Erdman, president of BT.Novations (the company that employs two of the authors), has been an enthusiastic sponsor and cheerleader. All of our colleagues—whether at the universities where we teach or the consulting firm where we work—have been wonderfully encouraging and helpful whenever asked.

We also want to thank artist Brian Kershisnik. His work chronicles the absurdities of the human condition but always with affection and humor. It seemed perfect for the cover of this book.

Finally, we must thank the numerous clients and friends who thoughtfully critiqued our ideas or invited us to test our findings within their organizations. Our only hope of repayment is that they find the book's ideas personally and organizationally useful.

AUTHORS' NOTE

We are extraordinarily grateful to the dozens of balance seekers whose voices appear in this book. In order to protect their privacy, we have in most cases changed their names and identifying characteristics.

PART ONE

The Age of Imbalance

I

A New Holy Grail

CHANDLER, ARIZONA, 5:30 A.M. The alarm coaxes Kate Henstrom out of a dream. She reaches over to nudge her spouse. Nothing but an empty pillow. "Oh yeah," she remembers, "it's that sales meeting in Orlando or somewhere." Which means Kate's on quadruple duty this morning: get the kids off to school and herself to her job at Intel and the house semitidy for the sitter and the car to its six-weeks-overdue emissions test, not necessarily in that order. She's starting to butter the toast when the phone rings. Her babysitter sounds tired: "Um, I've been sick all night and so I probably shouldn't come over today. I'm really sorry." "Great," Kate thinks. Now what? As she searches her Palm Pilot for the phone number of her backup childcare provider, the device chirps at her. Up pops an appointment reminder. She panics—the team meeting that starts in twenty minutes had slipped her mind.

Go ahead, admit it: Sometimes you feel your life is out of control. You yearn for a more satisfying mix of the professional and the personal. Both are important to you—you thrive on challenging, meaningful work, and at the same time you're trying to maintain those stimulating, "battery-charging" activities that are unrelated to your employment. Striking the right balance is the hard part. More often than not, you feel as though you're struggling—perhaps even failing—in both areas.

If so, you're in good company. In the work world of the new millennium, balance is emerging as the new career Holy Grail: universally coveted, rarely found. This represents a significant shift from the rallying cry of past generations of workers. For years, the tacit assumption was that most professionals, particularly those with highly specialized skills, were clawing as hard and as fast as they could toward the top of their career ladders. Their motivations were presumed to be the usual: power, money, fame, influence, status, security. Yet when today's hard-working professionals assess their career ambitions, a large (and growing) percentage put balance at the top of the list.

The statistics are striking:

- Ninety-seven percent of all workers say that the ability to balance work with nonwork pursuits is important in a job; 88 percent consider it very or extremely important—more important than job security, health and medical coverage, and total annual income.[1]

- In a recent study at IBM, inability to balance work and personal/family life was tied with compensation as the leading reason employees gave for why they might leave the company.[2]

- For the past decade, this book's authors have delivered career planning seminars in Fortune 500 companies. In the process, we've administered a simple assessment of career motives to more than 60,000 professionals. Balance is in first place by a landslide, registering as the dominant driver for more than 24,000 (40 percent) of these people. That's nearly twice as many votes as the second-place driver (security), not to mention the other choices (freedom, challenge, and advancement).[3]

Similar findings have led Sue Shellenbarger, author of the weekly "Work and Family" column in the *Wall Street Journal,* to observe, "For the first time, the desire to find balance between work and personal or family life is coming up in surveys as workers' top priority."[4]

So if you're feeling like your life is a treadmill and you can't find the stop button, rest assured that a lot of people are feeling the same way. Henry David Thoreau hit it on the head nearly 150 years ago: The mass of men (and women, we'll add) lead lives of "quiet desperation." Now, as then, the desperation revolves around the daily difficulty of making a living while still having a life.

Now for some good news. Work-life balance is not an impossible dream. Difficult, certainly. Fraught with trade-offs, no question. But over the past five years, we've talked to plenty of people who've found imperfect but workable solutions to the balance dilemma. They come from all walks of life, all age groups. Many are women, but an increasing number are men. Their incomes vary widely. Cutting across this diversity, however, is a striking similarity: The vast majority have realized that they won't achieve balance by running faster, working harder, and cramming more into their lives. They've let go of the idea of *juggling* everything.

This doesn't mean they've dropped out of society and are surviving on organic vegetables and goat's milk. (Not that there's anything wrong with that.) Voluntary simplicity works well for many people. But most of the successful balancers we've studied aren't interested in an extreme version of the simple life. They accept as a given that the three components of balance—rewarding work, deeply satisfying relationships, and rejuvenating self-care—rarely come together in a tidy, stress-free package. Aware of this tension, they employ a variety of strategies to *rebalance* their lives into a more satisfying—and sustainable—pattern.

This book will share with you their stories, explore the pros and cons of their decisions, and provide tools to help you determine which strategy (or strategies) will work best for you. None is a panacea; each requires tough choices. But if you're serious about achieving better balance in your life, we're convinced that the least promising approach is to grit your teeth and keep trying to do it all.

WHY WE JUGGLE

Few of us need to be reminded that our lives are periodically out of kilter. We hope the neighbors don't notice, but we each know what it's like to be stretched thin, to burn the candle at both ends, to fight to keep our heads above water. We are busy people in a busy society, getting more done than was once thought humanly possible. Corporations call this practice "doing more with less"; to individuals, it feels more like a cruel "good news, bad news" joke. The good news: Your company's downsizing, but you're keeping your job! The bad news: You're keeping Frank's and Sally's jobs, too.

You've probably seen the headlines: U.S. workers now spend longer hours on the job than do workers of any other industrialized nation. It averages out to almost 2,000 annual hours of labor—roughly a week per year more than we worked in 1990 and two and a half weeks more than in 1980. That's also two weeks per year more than the second-place Japanese and roughly twelve weeks (three full months!) more than the Germans.[5]

So why aren't we celebrating our global number-one ranking? Probably because we're too tired—not just from the extra work but from the game of catch-up we're playing in the rest of our lives. Do the math: You're spending more time on the job; what are you spending *less* time on? Exercise? Friendships? Vacations? Housework? Sleep? The likely answer is "all of the above—and more." It's easy to relate to Golda Meir's nightly inventory when she was prime minister of Israel: "Whom or what did I neglect today?"

This is not to paint work as the villain, embezzling its unsuspecting victims of their precious free time. On the contrary, engaging work is essential to a satisfying life. No one wants to be a drone. And the risks of unemployment or underemployment are significant (an argument we'll make strongly in the next chapter). Yet when paid work eclipses other personal endeavors, life feels lopsided—just as it would if a personal crisis thwarted a unique career opportunity.

In short, you don't need to apologize for "wanting it all"; it doesn't mean that you're greedy or obsessive or self-indulgent. Think of it as having broad interests or staying well-rounded. But there are only so many hours in a day, so much energy in a person. Work fast, work smart, multitask, eat breakfast in your car, have lunch at your desk, drink prodigious amounts of diet Coke, bring your mobile phone to Suzy's recital, answer voice mail and e-mail before you go to bed—and chances are you still won't get it all done.

Comedian Steve Wright has observed, in his inimitable deadpan, "You can't have everything. Where would you put it?" In our hearts, we know he's right. But that doesn't keep us from trying to pack everything in anyway. And when it doesn't quite fit, we turn to the only other option we're aware of: We juggle.

THE PROBLEM WITH JUGGLING

Forty-five minutes, two seconds.

That's the longest time that Anthony Gatto, juggler extraordinaire, has ever kept five clubs in the air. In fact, it's the longest anyone has. His feat at the 1989 Baltimore convention of the International Juggling Association is the world record. But add one more club, or two, and Anthony can't juggle much past a minute. Give him eight clubs and the best he has ever managed is twelve catches—technically a "flash," since a bona fide "juggle" requires touching each object at least twice.

Anthony's a professional juggler; most of us are not. But we're trying to do the same thing with six, seven, eight, or more simultaneous commitments: coaching Little League, managing a project team at work, caring for a mother with dementia, encouraging a child to practice the French horn, helping out with the 5K charity run, learning yoga, and simply getting a family clothed and fed.

Patti Manuel, the president and chief operating officer of Sprint Long-Distance, consciously identifies the roles in her life—her juggling props. "I'm a boss, an employee, a friend, a mother, a daughter, and a member of my church and community." (That's seven.) "Balance is about understanding what these roles are and not letting any one of them become dominant. Most of the time, I'm good at this. Other times, I'm trying to manage my way back from chaos."[6]

Patti is both aware of and articulate about the challenges of juggling. In contrast, few of us even realize we're doing it. Juggling is a knee-jerk coping mechanism, the default setting when time gets tight and it seems nothing can be put on the back burner. No sooner have we tossed one task up in the air than the next two plummet earthward, screaming for our attention. As long as our reflexes are sharp, it works; we can "have it all." For that forty-five minutes and two seconds—or one minute, or just twelve catches—we've got a challenging work life, a fulfilling relationship with a partner, quality time with our friends (or children or both), and sufficient snatches of personal rejuvenation. Then something happens—a child gets sick, a friend loses his job and needs our help, we get stuck in traffic—and it all comes crashing down around us.

This is the problem with juggling: It's high maintenance, complicated, and stressful. It yields days that are exciting and full of variety but also exhausting and tinged with regret ("Whom or what did I neglect?"). It is widely practiced, as people try to stay engaged in their profession and involved with multiple personal commitments and interests. But does it work?

BEYOND JUGGLING

We interviewed hundreds of people for this book. Most identified themselves as jugglers. Not surprisingly, few were satisfied with the results. As we talked to them, we started to hear a number of creative tactics and techniques for achieving balance *beyond juggling*. The more we heard, the more these tactics seemed to fall into five consistent categories. We have chosen to call each of these categories a "strategy" for work-life balance. Three of the alternative strategies—alternating, techflexing, and simplifying—usually require fundamental changes in people's work-life patterns. The other two—outsourcing and bundling—are approaches that can be applied to almost any life pattern. Allow us to briefly introduce these five strategies; later in the book we will study each more carefully.

ALTERNATING

This is a strategy in which work-life balance comes in separate, concentrated doses. Alternaters want it all but not all at once. For a period, they throw themselves into their careers with abandon. Then they cut way back (or quit work altogether) for a season and focus on their nonprofessional interests. They toggle between intensive focus on their work and intensive focus on nonwork life.

The alternater's shifting focus usually is according to a plan, but sometimes it's spontaneous. A young MBA graduate may give five years of her life to McKinsey & Co., then donate the next year to an inner-city youth literacy project. Many couples work feverishly for ten years to establish themselves, then become a one-paycheck household while their children are preschoolers. Another variation is the couple who "take turns": the man immerses himself in his career for three years while the woman accommodates, then they switch. Such an approach inevitably requires a kind of career down-shifting during certain periods—an implication to be addressed at length in chapter 3.

OUTSOURCING

"We have a family of four and a staff of eight," quips Joel Klein, a New Jersey–based management consultant. Between his travel schedule and his wife's full-time community work, the Kleins have precious little free time to allocate to a seemingly endless list of de-mands. Their solution: Carefully prioritize those activities in which they want to be personally involved, then find ways to hire out the rest. On the "personal" list are coaching children's sports, religious observances, quality time with extended family (grandparents, aunts and uncles, cousins), walking the dog, and one-on-one time with their two sons. Just about everything else—yard care, food prepa-ration, academic tutoring, vacation planning, car maintenance—gets outsourced.

Outsourcers achieve work-life balance by off-loading responsi-bilities—usually in their personal lives—to free up time and energy to inject more meaning into those areas they want to keep under their control. Their motto might be "I want to *have* it all, I just don't want to *do* it all myself." Outsourcers with limited disposable income rely on a robust network of reciprocal social support—friends, neighbors, relatives, or fellow church and club members who band together to help each other gain a bit of balance in their lives. As a bonus, they feel confident that the family/community help is higher quality than even the most pricey commercial services.

For those with more money than time, there's certainly no short-age of help for hire. Couple the complex demands of contemporary life with a relatively affluent society and—*Presto!*—all kinds of quirky new jobs are created: errand runners, bill payers, in-home karate tutors, piano-lesson-and-soccer-practice chauffeurs, thank-

you-note writers, gift buyers/wrappers/shippers, and personal train-
ers. Clearly, we are evolving into a society of outsourcers—and
many people use outsourcing to achieve balance, a trend we'll delve
into in chapter 4.

BUNDLING

Bundlers involve themselves in fewer activities, but they get more
mileage out of those activities. Rather than give up certain interests
altogether (like simplifiers do), they examine their busy lives and
look for areas where they can "double-dip." For example, a group
of women get together three mornings a week to work out. This
accomplishes an important goal for physical exercise, at the same
time providing regular social contact and deepening their ties of
friendship. Or a middle-aged father volunteers to be a scoutmaster
so that he can kill three birds with one stone: time with his sons,
community service, and communion with nature.

For many, this practice is second nature; everyone bundles to
some degree. However, bundling is much more than mere multitasking. It requires that you search for ways to invest life's tasks with
greater meaning—an approach we call *multipurposing*. This strategy
will be explored fully in chapter 5.

TECHFLEXING

It's a classic *New Yorker* cartoon: Three guys with fly-fishing rods
are in the middle of what looks like a Montana trout stream. One of
them is answering his cell phone: "Fenwick, Benton & Perkins.
How may I direct your call?"

This is the techflexers' dream—to leverage technology to the
point that they can conduct their work from almost anywhere, anytime. Not that they want to be working all the time. As implied by
its name, the key to this strategy isn't just technology but *flexibility*.

Techflexers have figured out how to maximize the control they have over their schedules. That Nokia phone clipped to their belt isn't just a status symbol or fashion accessory. It's an emancipator. The DSL line at home? A boundary minimizer.

In contrast to the jugglers, techflexers don't use technology to increase the work hours in a day. Rather, they use it to liberate those work hours from the rigid 8:00-to-5:00 structure, as well as to enrich their personal lives. This "e-topia" isn't for everyone. Neo-Luddites, for instance, need not apply. Nor is techflexing an option for people whose work requires access to specialized machinery, face-to-face meetings, or numerous brief interactions with peers or supervisors. But for those who've found the right formula (a number of whom we'll meet in chapter 6), technology is the cornerstone of their balanced lifestyle.

SIMPLIFYING

Simplifiers have decided they don't want it all. They've made a lasting commitment to reduce the time and energy devoted to "nonessential" activities, whether at work or at home. The pay-off, they hope, is greater freedom—from stress, from minutia, from the rat race.

In the physics of work-life balance, simplifying strikes us as an equal and opposite reaction to the craziness of juggling. It brings with it the likelihood of slower career advancement and less accumulation of material goods. Some people pursue this approach from the beginning of their careers; others come to this strategy after they've tried juggling for a while. In either case, a common characteristic is the will to make some sacrifices—small ones, like "I've decided to buy only one color of socks," or large ones, like "I took a voluntary pay cut and work only four days a week." We'll revisit this strategy in chapter 7.

REBALANCING YOUR LIFE

We began this chapter with the assertion that work-life balance is a reachable goal. This doesn't mean it's easy. All of the evidence suggests that the three elements of balance—work, relationships, and leisure—form an unstable compound. We have met few people who live in a perpetual state of blissful equilibrium. Like happiness, balance appears to be a journey, not a destination.

But we've seen countless creative and successful approaches by people who've *rebalanced* their lives. Among those determined to stop juggling, we found five alternative strategies for work-life balance: alternating, outsourcing, bundling, techflexing and simplifying. Each of the five encompasses a different set of choices. These strategies are not necessarily attractive—nor, in some cases, available—to all people. Nor are they often employed in isolation from one another. Rather, successful rebalancers use them in combination to stay on course toward their definition of work-life satisfaction. We've attempted to document faithfully the trade-offs and sacrifices these strategies require.

We find it helpful to think in terms of *rebalancing* our lives—a process that we never quite get right and yet never abandon and in which small changes can have a large impact. Work-life balance isn't an all-or-nothing phenomenon. It's incremental, played out at the margins of our lives, where an hour or two per week to spend on the activities that matter most to us can spell the difference between feeling out of control versus tired but satisfied.

The principal aim of the book is to assist you in your own efforts to rebalance your life. Specifically, we hope the book helps you achieve three objectives:

1. Understand the degree to which you currently juggle your work and nonwork lives and the reasons why you do.

2. Examine a set of viable alternatives to juggling, each with an aptitude test to help you gauge its applicability to your life and career.

3. Craft a plan for rebalancing your life in a way that will continue to yield greater enjoyment and fulfillment both on and off the job.

We'll turn our attention now to the first of these objectives: a brief review of the forces that have created a nation of jugglers.

2

A Nation of Jugglers

WITH HIS FAST-PACED WORK at a San Francisco-based realty investment firm, an hour commute each way, and an active young family, Todd Sterling freely admits there are times when his life is way too much. Here's what he considers a "normal" day: Go for a run at 5:00 A.M.; read the paper on the BART train to work; eat lunch at his desk; coach his seven-year-old son's soccer team in the evening; help his wife with the dishes; get the five-year-old twins ready for bed; do a bit more work on his home computer if he needs to; then, finally, collapse sometime between 10:00 and 11:00 P.M. But when he's traveling for business or working around the clock to close an important deal, "It's just a meltdown," he says. Exercise is the first thing to go. Next comes sleep. "During crunch times, I get about an hour or two a night," Todd says. "It's a mess for about a week; then I crash and have to recover afterwards."

Todd Sterling's life is highly pressured, packed tightly, teetering on the brink of chaos—and, as such, thoroughly unremarkable. A generation ago, a schedule as out of control as Todd's would have been considered abnormal, an exception. Now it's almost the rule for many people. What has happened to our society in the past thirty years? Why are we all rushing around? As noted in the previous chapter, we're working longer hours than ever—longer than any other industrialized nation. How, exactly, did we lose our balance?

OUR COLLECTIVE IMBALANCE

Two factors contribute strongly to our collective imbalance: the dramatic feminization of the workforce and the new economy's "work hard or fall behind" imperative. We'll examine these fundamental changes and their impact on our work-nonwork choices, showing how—like it or not—all roads lead to juggling.

THE FEMINIZATION OF THE WORKFORCE

The new economy is involving women as knowledge workers for the first time in substantial measure—not as substitute men (as during World War II), nor as mere clerical, administrative, or temporary workers (as in the post-war years). Consider these facts:

- Three out of four women between the ages of 20 and 54 are now in the labor force.[1]

- Despite continuing pay inequities and glass ceilings, 48 percent of working women are their family's principal breadwinners.[2]

- Women now earn 55 percent of the bachelor's degrees, 53 percent of the master's degrees, and 40 percent of the doctor's degrees in the United States. As a result, an even half of the professional and technical work force is female.[3]

- More than 60 percent of mothers with children under the age of six are in the work force; for mothers with children of all ages, the figure is 72 percent.[4]

- In two out of three couples with children under age 18, both parents work for pay.[5]

This change in gender roles has huge implications for work-life balance. First, working mothers—whether married or not—face unrelenting pressure to "do it all." For them, juggling is almost second nature, though it exacts a heavy toll on their health and well-being. Out of necessity, men whose wives work outside the home are getting more involved in homemaking and child rearing; 75 percent of men now report feeling torn between work and family demands. Husbands do 45 percent of household chores and spend two-thirds as much time as their wives with the children—not quite parity, but a decided shift from their parents' generation.[6] The result is that more fathers find themselves juggling as well.

Organizations are adapting to some degree. Women formerly had to manage their careers the "male" way, emphasizing work at all costs. Younger women are rejecting the "harried superwoman" model, however, in favor of a more satisfying integration of personal and professional life. They seek flexible schedules and other family-friendly benefits. Companies that want to attract and retain talented women in their executive, managerial, and professional ranks have little choice but to adopt progressive work-life policies. Balance-oriented men are the unintended beneficiaries. But change—in corporate programs and managers' attitudes—is slower than many people wish.

WORK HARD OR FALL BEHIND

In 1977, country singer Johnny Paycheck scored an unlikely number one hit with his song "Take This Job and Shove It!" A quarter-century later, people aren't feeling so cavalier about quitting, even though their job burdens continue to grow. The sentiment today is more akin to "Take This Job and Put It on Weight Watchers."

Those not among the 35 million or so laid off in the 1990s (and who've escaped the recent flurry of pink slips) find their knees buckling as they try to do the tasks formerly shared by two or three employees—not just in emergency bursts but as an ongoing job description.[7]

To be sure, fewer people doing equal or more work leads to increases in productivity. But higher productivity hasn't translated into greater job security. Corporate reorganizations and headcount reductions continue; "rightsizing" appears to be a never-ending process, like painting the Golden Gate Bridge. What's going on?

To quote Bill Clinton's 1992 campaign phrase, "It's the economy, stupid!" But it's an economy unlike any we've ever seen. Innovation is fueling new, better, and cheaper products and services. The Internet creates an incredibly efficient market for these goods, giving consumers almost infinite choice and eliminating the middle man. As a result, companies have to compete as never before, cutting costs to the bone and reinventing themselves to keep up with fast-changing consumer preferences. Political economist Robert Reich explains it like this:

> The emerging economy is offering unprecedented opportunities, an ever-expanding choice of terrific deals, fabulous products, good investments, and great jobs for people with the right talents and skills, [but] . . . the easier it is for us as buyers to switch to something better, the harder we as sellers have to scramble in order to keep every customer, hold every client, seize every opportunity, get every contract. As a result, our lives are more and more frenzied.
>
> The faster the economy changes, . . . the harder it is for people to be confident of what any of us will earn next year or even next month, what they will be doing, where they will be doing it. As a result, our lives are less predictable. . . .

For all of these reasons, most of us are working harder and more frantically than we did decades ago when these trends were just beginning, and than do citizens of other modern nations where these trends are not as far along.[8]

So much for the leisure society envisioned by futurists in the '60s and '70s. Reich makes a vital point: It's entirely *logical* that we feel a strong pull toward imbalance. Professionals with new-economy skills are in demand and making top dollar. Yet their jobs aren't secure—witness the "tech wreck" of 2001 and its aftermath. Workers without the "hot" skills are caught in a double bind: their wages are stagnating (in real dollar terms) *and* their jobs aren't secure. For many of these households, having two wage earners is a necessity, not a luxury.[9]

The economic imperative is clear: If you have a decent job, get all you can out of it and hold on to it. Slowing down or dropping out of the race are extremely risky options; the rational response is to keep running. So if you're feeling morally deficient because you find yourself tempted to work all the time, cut yourself some slack. You might as well feel guilty about the undertow, tugging at your legs as you stand, knee-deep, in the waves that wash up and down the beach.

THE PERSISTENCE OF VALUES

At the macro level of national (or global) economies, all of this individual hard work pays off in the form of higher output, greater return on investment, and growth in the GDP. These are undeniable benefits to society. Even for the most hyperextended individuals, this "busyness" has its rewards: professional growth, pride of accomplishment, and a measure of financial security and peer recognition. It also has its costs.

Chris Watson has an intellectually stimulating job as a management consultant, working with clients all over the world. Not yet thirty years old, she pulls down a six-figure income, keeps an apartment in New York, and vacations in such exotic locales as Bali and Cancun. She's competitive (a downhill skier on her college team), talented (plays guitar and sings in a Christian folk-rock group at her church), and attractive (tall, slender, and blonde). She has only one problem: "I'm never in one place long enough to build a meaningful relationship," she says. Although she has tried a couple of different dating services and has met a handful of promising men (among a truckload of duds), she confesses it's a turn-off when she tells them, "I'd love to go out with you again—how about two months from now, after I finish this project in Baltimore?"

Chris's story illustrates the tug-of-war that's playing out in a lot of people's lives. See if this sounds familiar: On the one hand, you enjoy your job. You feel needed (always), challenged (usually), and appreciated (well, two out of three's not bad). On the other hand, you long for more time with your partner, children, and/or close friends. While you're grateful for your employer's attempts to help you cope—flextime, telecommuting, cafeteria-style benefits, and on-site childcare—you still bring work worries home and domestic concerns to the office. You get a regular paycheck, but you rarely get enough sleep.

In other words, you're a normal, healthy, conflicted adult—and the conflict stems, in part, from the tension between your "internal" and "external" careers. As difficult as it is to manage one career, you're actually managing two simultaneously. Your internal career reflects your inner view of career and life success: what you find most satisfying, meaningful, and rewarding. In contrast, your external career consists of the job options and opportunities for a person with your background, skills, and training.[10] Both of these elements—

what you want and what's available—are important, though not always in synch.

During economic booms (like the late 1990s), employment choices are plentiful and people are freer to follow their inner compass. Many of the hottest jobs, however, require near-total commitment, which can impinge on internal career values. When the economic pendulum swings to recession and uncertainty, people often feel more constrained by the external career, grateful to have a job at all. Paradoxically, this also can be a time of reevaluation and renewed focus on "what's really important" (i.e., the internal career).

Given its persistence in good times and bad, we believe that the desire for balance is a widespread human characteristic—a part of most people's internal career values. Its intensity may vary, but the fact that you're reading this book suggests that, at present, work-life balance is on your internal career agenda. Life's unexpected trials, stock market gyrations, company layoffs, once-in-a-career opportunities, a sudden health crisis—these and myriad other unpredictable events—may keep you from achieving balance, but we doubt they'll prevent you from *wanting* it.

WORKAHOLICS, DOWNSHIFTERS, AND JUGGLERS

Individual choices around work-life balance, then, are shaped by two powerful and often conflicting forces: the siren call of the external career, offering rich rewards for hard work but promising little security in return; and the less seductive but more enduring voice of the internal career, whispering, "Follow your heart!" People respond to this tension in one of three ways: (1) they concentrate on their profession and minimize outside interests, (2) they subordinate professional life to the pursuit of nonwork goals, or (3) they try hard to maximize both. We'll explore each of these patterns in turn, focusing most on the last one, since it is a prescription for juggling.

PATTERN 1: ALL WORK, ALL THE TIME

You have to admire the single-mindedness of this approach. "My work is my life," goes the reasoning, "and I'm not going to worry too much about the other stuff." This sounds a lot like workaholism, but consider its advantages, articulated by columnist Donald Akst:

> The dogma of balance is fine as far as it goes, but it doesn't apply to everyone. For those committed to greatness, for instance, it should be anathema. For those who passionately love their work, it's a lot of guilt-inducing folderol. And even for the rest of us, it is rhetoric that doesn't quite equal the reality, because the world would be a lot poorer without people willing to throw themselves heart and soul into whatever they're doing.[11]

Akst's point is well taken. All work and no play make Jack a dull boy; then again, he might discover a cure for cancer. But he probably won't coach soccer, assuming he even marries or has children. Nor will he join a community bowling league or charitable service organization.[12] In this scenario, Jack has chosen to dedicate himself to his work, and it's a legitimate choice. It requires trade-offs, however, that many people are not willing to make.

PATTERN 2: WORK TO LIVE, NOT LIVE TO WORK

An equally legitimate but opposite choice is to back away from heavy involvement in your profession and pour yourself into your family, hobbies, and other interests. This doesn't mean quitting your job, unless you're independently wealthy. More typically, this choice involves stepping off the fast track, seeking a less intense (and usually lower paying) position, or arranging for part-time work.

It takes courage to attempt it and self-denial to follow through.

The rewards can be sweet, however. James Scripko and Nancy Greger each work part time, focusing their energies on family:

> To preserve lots of time with their children [ages 13, 11, and 8], the couple draw firm boundaries around it. They also draw firm limits on spending. They live in a cramped, 30-year-old, three-bedroom ranch house; drive two early-1990s Plymouths; and shun expensive vacations and eating out. Preparing for college costs, the couple saved more than one-quarter of their income last year. Mr. Scripko could make 40 percent more and Ms. Greger 20 percent by working full time. But "we'd rather have time over the money," she says.[13]

This couple's lifestyle has much in common with the voluntary simplicity movement. "Take back your life," it beckons. "Do less, and enjoy it more." It's an appealing message. By one estimate, about 12 percent of the population are now pursuing some type of scaled-down life (an approach we'll revisit in chapter 7). The extreme form of simplifying is not a work-life strategy for the masses, however.[14] Many people consider work a crucial variable in the balance equation; their lives would feel hollow without a significant and challenging occupation. For others, focusing on work is a matter of economics: They can't afford either the reduced paycheck or the opportunity costs associated with career downshifting.

"Someday, I might quit and teach high school," says Todd Sterling, the real estate investor profiled at the beginning of this chapter. "It would give me a more flexible schedule." But an educator's salary won't support his current standard of living in the pricey Bay Area. Unless he hits the jackpot on one of his deals—or is willing to move to Iowa or somewhere similar—he will probably never teach. In the meantime, he says, "I like my job. It's exciting. Every day is different. And I still have a great time with my kids." This is a perfect description of the third (and most common) work-life pattern.

PATTERN 3: WORK HARD, PLAY HARD

Nature (the human variety, at least) abhors a trade-off. Why be forced to choose our work over everything else or vice versa? We want—and feel that we deserve—both. Thomas Jefferson wrote that "life, liberty, and the pursuit of happiness" are among humankind's "unalienable rights." Work, family, friends, recreation, spirituality, community service—all of these make us happy. Is it any surprise that when asked whether we'd prefer a fully developed professional life or a rich and diverse personal life, most of us say yes?

Hence the popularity of juggling. Unless you're willing to cut back your involvement both at work and outside of work, you invariably find yourself overcommitted. This is not necessarily bad; it leads to a full and multifaceted life. It also wears you out. All four of the authors of this book are at least partial jugglers. We know firsthand that it's both exhilarating and exhausting, and we don't think it's sustainable. That's why the bulk of this book is about rebalancing our lives in order to do less juggling.

But make no mistake: Everyone juggles at some point. Let's see what we can learn from those who make the best of it.

CHARACTERISTICS OF SUCCESSFUL JUGGLERS

Some people have just the right mix of temperament and traits to gracefully juggle their way through life. They honestly seem to have it all, and they rarely appear to be out of control. If you've ever been backstage during a large-scale theatre production, however, you've witnessed the impeccably orchestrated mad rush that results in a smooth, well-timed performance. So it is with successful jugglers. It's not that their lives are less overloaded. Rather, they're careful about the logistics and, thus, keep a lot of the craziness behind the scenes.

HIGH ENERGY, HIGH STRESS TOLERANCE

Successful jugglers handle stress well, and their energy gets them through the crises that crop up. If their lives were aerobic workouts, they'd be the high-energy examples: full leg extensions, deep knee bends, and an extra hop in between. Todd Sterling, for example, would rather sleep on an airplane than sacrifice time with his kids. "I can't count the number of times I've taken a red-eye flight in order to be there for a game or a recital, and still make an East Coast meeting the next morning" he says.

Patti Manuel, in addition to her role as president and CEO of Sprint, spends one afternoon a week volunteering at her son's school. One of the ways she manages to fit all of these activities into a week is by capitalizing on her high energy. She sleeps only five hours a night.[15] Some would consider this strategy a serious compromise of personal health. Others would be willing to do it in short stretches but not as a lifestyle.

TIME MANAGEMENT

Setting priorities and managing your time effectively are basic skills for any busy professional, but jugglers go far beyond the baseline— and they do it all on the fly. "After all," comments a mother of two and vice president of shopping services at a New York City department store, "the juggler's trick is to respond to any changes in the breeze and to shift his or her weight accordingly to keep a balance."[16]

Jared and Monica Stewart are tenure-track assistant professors at the University of Oregon in Eugene—Monica is in marketing and Jared is in operations management. Their son, Sam, is eighteen months old. Both Jared and Monica are long-distance runners.

They believe that marriage is a partnership, and that parenting demands quality and quantity time from both parents. Yet they are also serious scholars; they don't want to cut corners on their teaching or do less than stellar research. Both Monica and Jared want a strong family life, but they also want academic success and the intellectual challenge that comes with it. The birth of Sam turned them into jugglers literally overnight.

They describe their juggling as "ad hoc and situational." Whoever is available deals with whatever needs to be done at the moment, with the understanding that the other partner owes some make-up time later. The person with the most urgent professional deadline has priority. So far, they haven't run into a situation that has been bigger than both of them or in which they felt the same crunch, but they know it's only a matter of time.

Sam is in the campus day-care center, which Jared describes as "Okay, but sort of minimalist." Besides, he says, "We want to be the adults that Sam spends his waking hours with." So they exploit the flexibility of academia to keep Sam's day-care stints at a minimum. They alternate who goes to work early and who comes home early. They consider the time after Sam's in bed to be golden work hours—if they can stay awake.

The Stewarts see this intensive juggling as a short-term strategy; they hope that the pressure will ease once Sam is older. But for now, the freedom of an academic schedule—and the discipline to manage their time carefully—make the juggling possible.

USE OF OTHER TECHNIQUES

Jared and Monica, like most jugglers, do whatever it takes at the moment (a little outsourcing, some techflexing) to keep the balls in the air. Both of them check in several times a day with each other by e-mail and voice mail; both carry mobile phones. Thanks to their jobs, they can afford a housecleaning service and Sam's day care. "But we struggle constantly with how much we can afford to spend in order to buy more time," says Jared. "We're always trying to figure out what trade-offs to make financially."

Todd and Jennifer Sterling have made a different trade-off: Jennifer has decided to be a stay-at-home mom right now. "She's with the kids the bulk of the day, shuttling them to and from school and sports," says Todd. "She does most of the cooking, though we hire a cleaning service and yard and pool maintenance to come once a week. For us to survive, she shoulders a lot of the grind at home." Todd is the first to acknowledge that, without such support, his life would spin out of control.

A MODICUM OF SELF-CARE

Skilled jugglers make sure to include some self-care in the mix. They think of themselves as long-term valuable resources who need ongoing maintenance and development—though they often want more than they get.

> Jill Blackham is an organizational effectiveness manager for a technology company that has become a household name. She routinely puts in the twelve-hour days that are the rule in Silicon Valley but faces an additional burden: Because she doesn't have a spouse or children, colleagues expect her to work even more. "They think I don't have anything else to do," she says. "That's not true. I've always had other interests."
>
> Jill, now 37, grew up in Colorado with exposure to a wide variety of activities. She maintains an active social schedule but finds little time for one of her deep loves, the outdoors. "I'm pretty good about seeing museums and taking in cultural events, but I miss the camping, hiking, and exploring national parks."

To lessen this imbalance, she has learned to trust her instincts and pay attention to her inner self. For example, she might have planned a Saturday full of errands when a friend will invite her to the beach. "I listen to what I really need and then act on it," she says. "Sometimes it's the beach, and sometimes it's the errands that win. It depends on the weather, my energy level, my mood, even things I can't put my finger on. But I've learned to listen to myself."

For Monica Stewart, long-distance running is what she craves—but it's been "pushed onto the back burner so far that it's practically off the stove," she says. "It takes an enormous amount of preparation just to get the logistics arranged to slip out for a quick jog, let alone the kind of systematic training that a long-distance event would take." Even so, the "quick jog" is sometimes just what she needs to clear her mind and restore her energy.

BY CIRCUMSTANCE, NOT CHOICE

So far, we've been profiling people who are jugglers by choice. Pulled by equally potent motivations from two directions—work and nonwork—they feel a powerful impulse to try to do it all. They need and want success in both areas of their lives. They are voluntary jugglers.

Many equally successful jugglers, however, can best be termed "involuntary." Their lifestyle may look like that of the voluntary juggler, but if they felt fewer constraints, they'd likely opt for a strategy like outsourcing, simplifying, or techflexing. Because of their life circumstances—such as intensive elder care obligations or marriage with a spouse who doesn't help at home—they see juggling as their only option.

Earlier in this chapter, we suggested that the feminization of the workforce has led to increased juggling—much of it involuntary.

Nowhere is this more apparent than with single mothers. They have demanding home responsibilities; they also have to work. They are educated, bright, and ambitious, and they push themselves incredibly hard to perform well in both arenas.

Meredith Long is a 26-year-old single mother in Seattle. She works for a recruiting firm as a customer service team leader, a position that brings her good pay and excellent benefits. She had her daughter, Jericho, when she was 21. The father has never had contact with the child, so Jericho's male role models are Meredith's brothers, both of whom live in the area. In the evenings, Meredith attends North Seattle Community College, where she's working on a degree in English.

She enjoys her work, but admits that it's not ideal. "I'd love to have more flexible hours," she says, "and the option of working from home a day or two per week." But as a team leader, she has to be in the office every day. She'd have more flexibility if she went back to a team member job, "but I can't afford the cut in pay," she explains. The next logical promotion is to a consulting role, but Meredith is clear she doesn't want it. "Consultants are never home long enough to pick up their dry cleaning," she says. "They're always out giving seminars or meeting with clients. It just wouldn't work with Jericho."

Meredith plans to use her degree to move into technical writing, a job that will give her more autonomy. In the meantime, she's caught in the middle. "I have to establish a good track record in this position so that I don't have to worry about job security," she says. "And I have to finish my degree before I can spiral off into another position." Her dream job would be as a part-time technical writer, working from home, with a spouse or partner who is employed full time.

She seeks balance in her life by doing things with Jericho, whose company she greatly enjoys, maintaining an exercise program, and spending time with friends. She loves her classes: "Getting this B.A. is like a hobby! I get to read all these great books—it's really stimulating." In fact, she thought about taking out a big loan and going full time. "But my company pays part of Jericho's childcare, part of my tuition, and my health benefits," she explains. "I couldn't afford to let go of all that."

How many Merediths are out there in the American workplace? Probably more than we think. The constraints are real. She has to make a good salary and have decent benefits. She will have few job options without a degree and more experience. A partner would both simplify and complicate her life. Will her dream of being a part-time writer working from home, with a partner and more children, come true? Maybe, but it's far from guaranteed.

WEIGHING THE TRADE-OFFS

As the case histories related above illustrate, juggling can be rewarding. The rewards come at a price, however. From your own experience, you're probably aware of juggling's downside captured on the brief list that follows:

DOING IT ALL, BUT NONE OF IT WELL

For people who want control over the various dimensions of their life or who find it exciting to keep many balls in the air, it is sometimes possible to perform an extraordinary feat of juggling. To be able to handle such complexity is self-enhancing, even if it is exhausting.

But if a juggler is a perfectionist, she learns to suppress it. Jill Blackham has to be content with not getting those errands done on

Saturday if she decides to go to the beach with her friend. Jugglers realize they are not going to excel in all areas, maybe not even in one. Because their desires and responsibilities are spread so broadly, "good enough" becomes the standard to shoot for in many areas.

STAYING IN THE GAME, BUT FEELING BURNED OUT

Doing it all in the short term may allow you to get over a busy hump so you can stay on a high-stakes career path or start a family. Monica and Jared are definitely holding their breath and tunneling through until Sam's a bit older. At least, they point out, neither has to lose a tenure-track position.

But the juggler's approach to work-life balance overwhelms many. That's why the other strategies we'll explore in this book have emerged. Some people don't have the health, the drive, the support, or the organizational energy for the high-intensity labor that juggling requires.

SATISFACTION VERSUS STRESS

Juggling is never boring. A lot of people like the variety; they find the process of juggling tiring but stimulating. They take pride in their ability to creatively manage such a breadth of activities. While they may fall short, they feel the challenge is its own reward and they accomplish much more than they would otherwise.

Yet even the most deliberate jugglers say that stress is a genuine hazard of their chosen approach. Things seldom go smoothly. A deadline at work, a childcare crisis (or a child in crisis), a fight with one's spouse, a spell of ill health—any of these minor emergencies can be the proverbial last straw, tipping the careful arrangements into chaos.

Jared and Monica Stewart know that if two crunches happen at once—they each have a tenure review, the childcare falls through, and the exam results have to be in—something will crash. As it is, the stress takes its toll.

"We ignore each other a lot more," sighs Monica. "We have less quality time. We're less patient with each other. We split up things that we used to do together because the point isn't to spend time together anymore—it's just to get the job done."

They rate their marital happiness at perhaps six on a ten-point scale. They often feel exhausted, frustrated, unsuccessful, and uncertain about the future. Part of their frustration comes from the mixed messages they're getting.

"The university offers these advantages of day care and flexible hours, but it penalizes you if you use them," observes Jared. "We'll probably never get as far as fast as some of our colleagues who put their careers first and devil take the hindmost, but we are really committed to doing it this way. We both want careers we can make contributions to and be happy at; we both want a shared marriage; and we both want to be involved parents. That's our definition of success."

So what is the Stewarts' advice about juggling? First, they say, understand that balance isn't free. You have to give something up to get something. They're sacrificing their fitness, some of their "couple" time, and rapid career advancement, in order to have Sam and stay involved in their professions. "By definition, juggling means that life isn't perfect in any one dimension," concludes Monica. "You just hope that it's worth it."

SUMMARY

On the road to a rich, full life, most people find themselves juggling competing demands on multiple fronts. A fast-paced, unpredictable economy demands ever-longer work hours, but individual workers still place high value on personal and family needs. Juggling is the only way they see to reconcile the two.

At the same time, few people have the stamina to juggle for the long haul. It exacts a heavy toll: stress, fatigue, burn-out, guilt. Consider these cautionary words from Brian G. Dyson, Vice Chairman and COO of Coca-Cola, at Georgia Tech's 1991 commencement:

> Imagine life as a game in which you are juggling some five balls in the air. You name them—work, family, health, friends, and spirit—and you're keeping all of these in the air. You will soon understand that work is a rubber ball. If you drop it, it will bounce back. But the other four balls—family, health, friends and spirit—are made of glass. If you drop one of these, they will be irrevocably scuffed, marked, nicked, damaged or even shattered. They will never be the same.[17]

What, then, is the solution? Is it too much to hope for a challenging career, meaningful relationships, and rewarding personal interests—at the same time? Has life for the dedicated post-modern careerist been reduced to "You're born, you juggle, then you die"?

Of course not. When an irresistible force (economic necessity) meets an immovable object (deep-seated personal values), incredible energy is released. Some of that energy dissipates as friction (individual frustration, anger, even despair). But a significant portion of it remains to be harnessed for productive use (innovative alternative approaches to work-life balance). We are now ready to turn our focus to these other work-life balance strategies.

PART TWO
Beyond Juggling

3

Alternating

MARK HAMMOND scrolled through the calendar on his computer, perusing his upcoming commitments. "What a relief," he said out loud, "nothing major for the next three months!" A human resource manager in a large pharmaceutical company, Mark had just finished an exciting but intense year-long project. It had sealed his reputation as a hard worker and bright thinker in his new company, but it had also exacted a toll. He was burned out. The project had pulled him away from his family and from his other great love, the outdoors, and he was ready to get back to them.

Of course, "nothing major" is a relative term. Mark has business trips to Italy and Shanghai penciled in, as well as a consistent schedule of leadership development sessions and organization design team meetings. But none of that seems too stressful to him. He won't be cramming at night to prepare for the next day—a pleasant change from the grind he's kept up for the last year. And he is actually looking forward to the international trips. Shanghai seems exotic and unusual; in Italy, his wife will join him, and they'll spend a few extra days touring Sicily. Overall, it will be a good time to recharge.

Mark is good at knowing how and when to recharge. Before this hectic first year with the pharmaceutical firm, he had spent six weeks of deliberate, therapeutic unemployment. "I was a full-time mountain biker and dad," he says. "It felt great to start the new job in fantastic shape, emotionally and physically. I was ready to sink my teeth into some challenging work." Now, after twelve months of job excitement, he was ready for downtime again.

Mark is an expert at alternating, a rebalancing strategy characterized by a series of intense work periods, followed by breaks to recharge. He's been doing it his whole career. Right out of college, he joined a then Big Eight accounting firm in his hometown of Calgary. The demands placed on new associates in the firm were steep—they were not only expected to carry a full load of billable client work but also use their "spare" time to prepare for the rigorous Chartered Accountant exam—the Canadian CPA equivalent. Mark managed to keep his sanity because the firm also allowed associates to bank their overtime hours. At the end of the first year, he had saved up nine weeks of overtime. He took the weeks off, spending six hours a day preparing for the exam, and spending the rest of the time with his wife, young son, and the rest of their large extended family.

In the twelve years since, Mark has alternated between full-time jobs, graduate school, contract work, and new business ventures, with almost every job change punctuated by a period of no work at all. "It's kind of a crazy lifestyle," he admits, "but it's allowed me to try a lot of different things. I like the intensity of demanding work. Whenever I've been away from work for extended periods of time, I eventually reach a point where I can't wait to get back. But I've also really savored the times that have allowed me to regroup and experiment with what I might like to do next."

HAVING IT ALL, BUT NOT ALL AT THE SAME TIME

Mark's roller-coaster approach is much more feasible in the twenty-first century than it might have been for previous generations. Today's perpetual downsizings and the death of corporate loyalty make flexible careers far more acceptable, sometimes even required. As a result, many people find themselves taking their balance in concentrated doses, with work taking a back seat at times and dominating their lives at others.

In some ways, alternating has grown in popularity because of sweeping organizational changes in the last fifteen years. In the old days, most jobs had periods of built-in downtime when professionals were waiting for the next project or assignment to come along—and assignments varied in intensity, which meant that some were more demanding than others. As organizations have worked to eliminate slack resources, intensity has become a constant for many careerists. As a result, a growing number of people actively take breaks, either on the job or by changing jobs. Others negotiate for fewer responsibilities or more flexibility in their work in order to meet growing nonwork demands or recover from periods of high stress.

More than a decade ago, Felice Schwartz identified one obvious group of alternaters in a controversial *Harvard Business Review* article. She juxtaposed the "career-family woman," who temporarily plateaus or leaves the workforce in order to meet increasing family demands, against the "career primary woman," who often sacrifices family or other personal commitments in order to focus primarily on her career. The article sparked a lively debate in the popular business press about the perils of the Mommy Track in light of the traditional "up or out" career strategy. Yet career-family women are now a larger group and more influential than ever.[1] Their struggles in alternating meeting family demands with pursuing career success have opened up opportunities for all professionals to consider broader options.

Jane Elmore joined a small consulting company fresh out of graduate school in the late 1980s. After five years of hard work, she became a partner in the firm. Her husband, Jack, is a part-time emergency room physician, as well as an aspiring screenwriter. The couple adopted an alternating strategy early on—Jack took a year off between medical school and his residency and devoted the first six months to hiking, camping, mountain biking, and general recovery. Jane took a leave of absence from her job for the second six months of Jack's break. They bought around-the-world plane tickets and immersed themselves in various corners of Asia for half a year. Later, when their first child was born, Jane took a six-month unpaid maternity leave (while Jack worked more intensively to make up for Jane's reduction in income); when her leave ended, Jane opted to work three days a week. "I wanted the part-time option to work out," she remembers, "but it was hard to do consulting work without a full-time commitment. Clients wanted whatever time I had available, and my partners seemed to expect a bigger commitment even though my compensation had been cut back to reflect my schedule."

Jane remembers a particularly unbalanced period of several months: "I was working on a project in New Jersey—and we were living in Los Angeles. I'd fly to Newark every Monday morning (or sometimes late Sunday night) leaving Jack home with our daughter, Emma. When flights went smoothly, I'd arrive back at LAX on Friday night at 8:30. Jack and Emma would pick me up at the airport, and we'd drive to the hospital, where I would drop Jack off to begin a 24-hour shift in the

ER. I'd spend Saturday with Emma (and recovering from a week of travel and work), and Jack would come home late Saturday night. He'd crash after such an intensive shift, and then emerge midday Sunday. We usually went to church together on Sunday afternoon, and then the cycle started over again—I'd be back on a plane. It became clear that this wasn't a sustainable way to live."

After trying to make the part-time consulting work for several years (and after the birth of their second daughter), Jane and Jack decided to make a dramatic lifestyle change. They moved to Salt Lake City, bought a home with a far lower mortgage payment than they could have found in Los Angeles, and Jane resigned from the consulting firm. "I realized that Emma would start school in a year or two. I thought it would be a lot easier to get to know her when she was four than when she was in high school."

While she still worked part-time starting a new business, Jane took advantage of her flexible and diminished work hours to take midweek outings with the girls and plan extended getaways to the family ranch. Once her new business—a Web-based tool to improve negotiating skills across an organization—started picking up speed, Jane returned to work full-time. This time, however, her home office allows her to work at odd hours so she can spend more time with the girls.

Although women who spend some time on the Mommy Track are good examples of alternaters, they aren't by any means the only professionals who use this strategy. An alternating strategy works well for people who want it all but who recognize that they can't have all of everything at the same time. They make continual trade-offs to maximize one experience at a time, rather than trying to juggle all experiences in concert.

Although alternating poses some obvious challenges in terms of consistent cash flow, it also offers the following advantages over other strategies discussed in this book:

- Alternating is a great strategy for people who like pouring themselves completely into a particular activity, whether in their work or in their personal life. In comparison to outsourcing, bundling, and juggling, alternating allows people to drink deeply and enjoy the "pure" experience of something before immersing themselves in something else.

- Alternating allows individuals to manage work demands around the changing demands of family or personal life. Toddlers take more of their parents' in-home hours than teenagers do; caring for elderly parents may become an issue in midcareer, but may not be a factor in early or late career.

- Alternating can be a way to recover from burn-out relatively quickly, and it may be a good rebalancing strategy for those who have a hard time setting boundaries around work they are passionate about.

- Alternating appeals to people who want to try a variety of career approaches or options; as long as they main-tain marketable skills, they aren't tied to a single employer or industry.

In this chapter, we'll take a look at a variety of professionals who have used alternating as a primary strategy and identify some keys and trade-offs for using it successfully. The following Alternating Aptitude Test will give you some insight into whether this is a viable strategy for you.

Alternating Aptitude Test

Place a check mark next to each statement that you believe is true for you.

_____ 1. My organization or profession provides a wide variety of possible assignments, which require varying levels of intensity or commitment.

_____ 2. My profession has built-in cycles of intense work time followed by substantial downtime.

✓ 3. I am disciplined about saving money and am comfortable living below my means.

_____ 4. I have a partner or spouse who is willing and able to alternate the primary breadwinner role with me.

_____ 5. I have highly marketable skills that would be valuable to many different companies (or that companies need badly enough to accommodate with flexible career approaches).

_____ 6. I have enough confidence in my abilities to either negotiate flexibility with my employer or to know that I can find new opportunities if I leave my current job.

_____ 7. I am able to keep current in my profession, even during periods when I am less engaged in work.

✓ 8. I am comfortable with uncertainty; it doesn't bother me to not know what lies down the road in a year or two.

_____ 9. I am good at building and maintaining personal and professional relationships, even with people that I might not be involved with on a regular basis.

(Continued)

> *Alternating Aptitude Test, continued*
>
> ___ 10. I can alternate work commitments and personal com-
>   mitments without too much negative impact on fam-
>   ily or significant others.
>
> ---
>
> *Scoring:* Count up the number of check marks you have made. Interpret
> your scores according to the following rules:
>
> **1–3 check marks:**   Alternating probably will not be your most effec-
>   tive strategy for work-life balance.
>
> **4–6 check marks:**   You should at least consider alternating as a strategy.
>
> **7–10 check marks:** Alternating is a strategy that may work extremely
>   well for you in your quest to rebalance your life.

CHARACTERISTICS OF SUCCESSFUL ALTERNATERS

FINDING THE RIGHT PROFESSION OR ORGANIZATION (QUESTIONS 1 AND 2)

Alternating is easy if your organization or profession already enables
an on-off schedule—periods of intense work followed by career or
workload breaks. In some occupations, such peak-and-valley intervals are built in. Tax accountants, for example, work incredibly long
hours during the first three and a half months of the year and then
have significant downtime. Retail, school teaching, and professional
sports jobs also have intervals of rest hardwired into the job.

> Max Bridger, a drilling foreman for a major petroleum company,
> works twenty-eight straight days of twelve-hour shifts on the
> rig he's assigned to in Egypt and then flies home to Louisiana
> for twenty-eight days. "This on-and-off schedule drives some
> guys crazy," Max says, "but it suits me just fine. While I'm on

the rig, I'm busy and focused—never a dull moment. When I
fly home, I leave work on the other side of the world. My wife
loves it because I'm completely at her disposal for almost a
month at a time, and it's great to have the golf course or fishing hole to myself on weekdays while everyone else is at the
office."

Mark Hammond (introduced at the beginning of this chapter)
resigned from the first three jobs on his resume because he wanted
a break from the intensity of work. Those early jobs were with small
companies that couldn't tolerate extended periods of downtime or
with companies that had highly competitive environments where
new associates were "up or out." Mark burned out after pouring
himself completely into his first few projects. He quit in order to sal-
vage his sanity.

Mark's current employer still has high performance expectations, yet the variety of possible assignments is much greater than
with a small or highly focused firm. "My current projects give me
the luxury of being able to do a great job while also recharging a little," he notes. "After a few months, I'll be ready to move back into
something more intense where my learning curve is steeper." Mark
also added that he expects to stay with this firm for at least ten
years, while he couldn't stay at any of the others for longer than
three years. "This company really goes out of its way to let people
recharge. Employees can take up to two years of unpaid leave without losing any of their health or retirement benefits. It makes it relatively easy for people to take sabbaticals."

If you aren't lucky enough to work in an occupation or for an
organization that makes alternating easy or even automatic, there's
still hope of using this strategy without quitting your job. Work hard
to establish your value to the organization; it will give you some
power to negotiate. For example, many professionals have used their
track record to trade continuing loyalty for flexible schedules or

leaves of absence. Depending on your profession and organization, this might mean working four ten-hour days each week and preserving the three-day weekend for nonwork priorities. Or it might mean taking an extended sabbatical with the promise of a job when you return.

EFFECTIVE FINANCIAL MANAGEMENT (QUESTIONS 3 THROUGH 5)

Another skill common to the alternaters we studied was financial prudence. They had an ability to manage their personal resources conservatively—on both the income and expense side. Off-and-on workloads almost always mean paycheck peaks and valleys. Working less time usually means either foregoing a future raise or even taking a hefty pay cut. And leaving a job completely means an abruptly dry financial well.

Mark Hammond has carefully planned his transitions from work to nonwork. "When I was with the large accounting firm and again when I left a small firm after graduate school, I was able to negotiate short-term contract work arrangements, where I traded off long-term job security for a much higher hourly or daily rate. At rates of up to $1,000 per day, I could put money away pretty quickly, especially because we had no nonmortgage debt and we'd kept our monthly house payment under $500. I also paid attention to tax issues. In one case, I did most of the contract work at the end of the calendar year. My former employer deferred payment to me until January. Since I didn't work full time for the rest of the year, I paid next to nothing in income taxes."

Jane Elmore has been able to alternate in and out of work because she and Jack have saved consistently. They've also made an investment in education that allows them to earn relatively high wages in a comparatively short amount of time. "Jack's years of medical training weren't easy," Jane notes, "and he decided at the end of his residency that he didn't want to practice full time. He wouldn't be able to pursue what he really wants to do—write screenplays—if he didn't have a high-paying part-time job."

Alternating is relatively easy for entrepreneurs who've made it or the lucky few who've cashed in generous stock options. With a nest egg put away that could conceivably last a lifetime, these individuals pick and choose where and how they work.

Wayne Chen was one of the first computer geeks in his high school. In the early 1980s, he started a software company with one of his classmates and then worked furiously for ten years to build a small but thriving business. When the two sold the company to a Fortune 500 company, Wayne garnered a modest fortune.

"I realized that I could easily live the rest of my life on what we got from the sale," he says. "So after a few months under the new management, I resigned. I'd worked eighteen hours a day for a decade, and I woke up one morning and realized that I literally had no life outside of work. My siblings were all married and had kids that I didn't even know, even though they all lived in the same city. I think it had been about six years since I had been on an actual date, much less had any kind of serious relationship."

Wayne spent the next few years catching up. He traveled extensively: "I had about a million frequent flyer miles saved up from all the flying I did to start the business," he laughs. He invested the time to nurture a healthy relationship with his girlfriend, Lisa. He also spent time learning about and playing with the latest technology—no pressure, just for fun.

After a two-year break, Wayne accepted a job as chief technology officer with a budding Internet business. "I'm being more careful this time to set some realistic boundaries so that I can still have a personal life," he said. "And I'm here because it's fun. When the fun runs out, I'll take another break."

Wayne's freedom is due to his economic windfall, but it wouldn't last long if he adopted a lavish lifestyle. "I drive a seven-year-old Honda and live in a two-bedroom condo, in a nice but definitely not luxurious neighborhood. It's not that I'm excessively cheap; if I married someone who wanted an expensive car or a nicer house, I wouldn't hesitate to buy them. I consider myself lucky to have simple tastes, and I like the idea that minimal financial commitments mean that I can do anything with my life."

Another option for successful alternating is available to two-career couples who are willing to take turns as the primary bread-winner. Bridget Jackson is a state supreme court justice, and her husband, Byron, is a pediatrician who has not only built a success-ful practice but who has also researched and published extensively. From outward appearances, both partners seem clearly committed to their careers. Both have certainly achieved remarkable levels of success. However, they've also balanced personal needs by taking turns focusing on their family.

Bridget finished law school and established herself as a young attorney while Byron completed his internship and residency. Their first child was born soon after Byron started practicing. Because he was fully engaged in building a professional reputation and Bridget had already firmly established credibility, she scaled back at work, reducing both her hours and her income by fifty percent.

Once his pediatrics practice was up and going, it became clear that Bridget had the potential to achieve her long-term goal of being appointed to a judgeship. Even though all three of their children were in school by this time, both felt that it was important to have a strong parental presence at home. Byron stopped accepting new patients and focused more on the family while Bridget reengaged professionally. Once she had received her appointment, they traded roles once again. Although reduced childcare commitments allowed both of them to work full time at this point, Bridget managed her schedule so she had plenty of time for their teenagers while Byron started a major new research project.

Either partner in the Jacksons' marriage could have solely supported the family financially with comfort to spare. However, without mutual support and a willingness to trade off, neither could have made the temporary career downshifts that both made without straining the family's budget. The teamwork approach allowed them to have satisfying careers and play a strong parenting role—a high priority for both of them. Jane and Jack Elmore take a similar approach, even though Jane is most often the primary provider. They trade off weekly or monthly, rather than in multiyear segments. "We sit down with our calendars on a regular basis and look out over several months. This year, my business has done very well, which has enabled Jack to work less at the hospital and more on his screenplays." When they have another child (pending at the time of this writing), Jack will increase his time at the hospital so that Jane can take some time off.

BUILDING PROFESSIONAL CREDIBILITY AND EQUITY (QUESTIONS 6 AND 7)

Alternating is an uncomfortable strategy for professionals who don't have a lot of confidence in their capabilities. "One reason I don't worry much about money," says Wayne Chen, "is that I know I can always make more. I have a rare combination of skills: a deep understanding of all kinds of information technology—as much a hobby as a profession—plus a hands-on understanding of how to take the technology to market and make money. That combination of skills won't go out of fashion anytime soon."

Similarly, Jane Elmore sees her investment in education and work experience as a key to pursuing multiple options. "Our oldest daughter was born when I was in my early 30s," she says. "If she had been born ten years earlier, I wouldn't have had time to establish a reputation and build a network. I wouldn't have had as many options if I had tried to make a lifestyle change early on."

The successful alternaters we spoke with all had a commitment to professional excellence, which they manifested in a willingness to invest in their own learning, even during the slow times. Knowing that they had a reputation and a large toolbox of skills to draw on gave them the self-assurance to be able to find new jobs or to be able to negotiate reduced commitments with the same employer. Mark Hammond can always find more work and succeed in new jobs because he has an established track record in a variety of areas. The Jacksons, the judge-pediatrician couple, both have remarkable professional achievements to their credit, despite having periodically put less emphasis on their careers. That wouldn't have happened if they had allowed themselves to fall behind during the times when they were less engaged.

MANAGING RELATIONSHIPS (QUESTIONS 8 THROUGH 10)

Just as financial inconsistency is part and parcel of alternating, so is the variable intensity of relationships. Managing career networks, family relationships, and friendships while living a feast-or-famine lifestyle takes commitment and skill. Alternating can be trying in and of itself. "People wonder how my marriage has survived for twenty years while I've been working rotating shifts," says Max Bridger, the drilling foreman who spends every other month overseas. "It hasn't been easy. My wife is fairly independent and is busy with her own career as a teacher. But she still gets lonely and feels like a single mother during the months that I'm gone. I've missed more than my share of science fairs and soccer games—not to mention birthdays and anniversaries. I just do my best to make up for what I've missed when I get home. I think it takes an extra measure of commitment to make sure the time at home is well spent."

Mark Hammond points out that spending intense time at work isn't the only challenge. "My wife's personality is almost the complete opposite of mine. She likes order, structure, and predictability. Although she was a successful business owner before we were married, we've done whatever we could to allow her to stay home full time while our kids are young. My tendency to take extended breaks from work hasn't done much to foster long-term clarity or security, and sometimes she feels like she doesn't have much control over her own destiny. We've had to work hard on our relationship to make sure we get through the times of uncertainty, when neither of us is at all clear what we're going to do next or when we might have a consistent income."

In cases where partners alternate primary breadwinner roles, alternating often means a certain amount of self-sacrifice. "There were times when it made sense from a family perspective for me to pull back professionally for a time," said Bridget Jackson, "even though those were often the times when I could have made great career strides if I'd taken a more selfish approach. We've really had to be disciplined about taking a long-term view, and that wouldn't have worked if we hadn't always thought of ourselves as a team first. The approach we've taken also wouldn't have worked if we'd allowed ourselves to feel competitive with each other."

Managing the expectations of people outside the couple or the family may also be a challenge. "Our friends and relatives haven't always been very enthusiastic when I was not working full time," says Mark Hammond. "My wife has been generally supportive, but other people had more traditional expectations about what I ought to be doing." Jane Elmore has had similar experiences as she and Jack have alternated roles. "I was in Chicago one week when Jack's aunt called me at my hotel. She had called Jack to get my phone number. Turns out she wanted to tell me what food to bring to the family dinner that Sunday. It never occurred to her that Jack was doing the shopping and the cooking that week, so I called him back to pass the message along."

Maintaining professional connections can be equally difficult during times of reduced work intensity, a challenge faced by Jane Elmore. "When I've been away from work—both when my daughters were born and when I left work completely for a while—I knew that I'd eventually go back to work full time. I also knew that one of my most valuable professional assets was my network of contacts. I worked hard to make sure that I didn't burn any bridges, always made sure I was giving the company full measure, and went out of my way to stay in touch with my circle of professional friends."

For those who attempt to alternate within a single organization, the political aspects of a variable commitment may be equally challenging. Managers may hesitate to invest in professionals who are seen as being less than fully committed, which may limit the development opportunities for alternaters. The red flags that Felice Schwartz raised about career-family women (who take a reduced role in the organization or leave altogether) apply to any alternater: the vast majority of companies prefer employees who are willing to give their all, all of the time. Although less substantial commitments are being tolerated more often as the talent pool shrinks, managing relationships within the organization means helping others see the benefit of accommodating an alternater.

WEIGHING THE TRADE-OFFS

The relationship management aspects of alternating also point to the challenges and trade-offs inherent in this strategy. If you're considering some variation of alternating to rebalance your life, go in with your eyes wide open.

LONG-TERM FINANCIAL SECURITY VERSUS CAREER FLEXIBILITY

Alternating doesn't work well for those with lavish tastes. The alternaters we interviewed all agreed that a modest lifestyle was key to buying career flexibility. Most felt it important to save for a (sometimes self-induced) rainy day, which gave them freedom to make risky choices when they couldn't necessarily see very far ahead.

"There was a time when we completely ran out of money," Mark Hammond reflects. "I had started a new business that wasn't as successful as I had hoped it would be. I learned a lot from the experience, but from a financial point of view, it was frightening. We had to take out a second mortgage on our home. Fortunately, I found a new job soon after that experience. If we hadn't lived carefully my whole career, saving whenever we could and maintaining an excellent credit rating, we wouldn't have had the option of taking that risk."

INTENSITY VERSUS MODERATION

Unlike professionals who rely primarily on bundling or juggling, alternaters don't pretend to pay attention to all of their priorities on a consistent basis. Although they try to compensate by being fully present at whatever they are engaged in at the moment, there's still a price to be paid. "I missed out on a lot of things that most people do in their 20s and 30s," Wayne Chen observes. "College wasn't as much fun for me as it was for a lot of students, because I was trying to start the business while working on my degree. I ultimately ended up dropping out, and I worry that my education is really unbalanced—technology and business are really the only things I know much about. I also missed out on a lot of the social aspects of being a young adult. If I eventually get married and have children, I'll be an old dad—over forty when my first child is born. I wonder if I'll have the stamina and energy my kids deserve."

ORGANIZATIONAL INFLUENCE VERSUS PERSONAL FREEDOM

Alternaters choose charting their own course over building leadership and influence in a single organization. In today's flatter organizations, the path to management is narrower and more crowded than ever before. Building informal influence usually requires the type of consistent effort that might not be an option for alternaters. "I'm in a big company now, for the first time in my career," says Mark Hammond. "It doesn't make sense for me to try to make it to the top of the corporate ladder—I got a much later start in this kind of career, and most people my age who were going to move up have already been promoted."

SUMMARY

Alternating is a rebalancing strategy that involves toggling between periods of intense work and intense nonwork. While it has its risks, alternating offers the luxury of single-minded focus without sacrificing balance. Those who use it successfully seem to have several qualities in common:

- An ability to generate a substantial income and/or live frugally

- A high tolerance for ambiguity and uncertainty

- An ability to effectively manage both professional and personal relationships, even when they aren't engaged with significant others for long periods of time

- A commitment to maintaining professional credibility and capability, even when work is not their primary agenda

This chapter has highlighted the careers of pure alternaters—individuals who use this strategy almost to an extreme. However, these cases should also provide ideas on how to exercise alternating in moderation, without a major career overhaul.

Ideas for Moderate Alternating

- Negotiate compensation/free time trade-offs.

- Occasionally take on less intensive assignments.

- Redefine career success in terms other than upward advancement in a single organization.

- Look for natural shifts in intensity, such as seasonal breaks or slow periods, and take advantage of those breaks to recharge or regroup.

- Use all of your holiday and vacation time, every year, for meaningful nonwork activities.

4

Outsourcing

"Can you believe it?" laughs Chris Watson (who was introduced briefly in chapter 2). "ConEd thought I was an imaginary person! I've never cooked a meal on my stove, never even turned on my oven. As far as they know, I don't really exist. I don't know why I bothered getting the gas connected in the first place. The building has central heat and hot water. I guess I have this dream that some day I'll find time to bake a batch of cookies."

Chris is a management consultant who lives in an apartment on Manhattan's Upper East Side. She loves her work. Even the travel is energizing, and the frequent flyer miles come in handy for exotic vacations. She is equally committed to her personal life and spends many weekends as a volunteer youth counselor for the Fifth Avenue Presbyterian Church of New York.

So when does she find time to do her wash, clean the apartment, prepare meals, and keep up an active social life? She doesn't. She deliberately hires out these services and focuses her discretionary energy on the few activities that are most important to her.

HAVING IT ALL VERSUS DOING IT ALL

The term "outsourcing" has worked its way into business lingo during the past decade, as corporations have slashed costs and reorganized around their "core competencies"—the activities and expertise that make them unique and differentiate them in the market. Nonstrategic activities have been spun off to suppliers, contractors, or vendors. It's hardly surprising that this exact process has been mimicked by individual workers as they strive to get control of their overstuffed lives. They outsource by farming out certain tasks and obligations (usually in their nonwork lives), then focusing more attention on the activities, relationships, and causes they care most about. As mentioned in chapter 1, their motto might be, "I want to *have* it all; I just don't want to (or can't) *do* it all myself."

Granted, everyone outsources to some degree. Since the time of the industrial revolution, our civilization has grown dependent on people's ability to buy many of life's basic necessities—food, clothing, shelter, transportation—rather than supply these goods for themselves. That's not what we mean by outsourcing in this chapter, however. As a strategy for rebalancing, outsourcing goes a bit beyond what most people consider normal. Chris Watson, for example, doesn't own a single piece of cookware. Nor does she own a car (not uncommon for a New Yorker). Instead, she pays others to prepare and clean up from her meals (in restaurants or via take out). Getting from point A to point B is a matter of subway trains, buses, cabs, and the occasional visit to a Hertz or Avis counter.

A recent *Fast Company* survey attempted to measure what people see as "normal" outgrowths of success and when such lifestyle factors cross the line to excessive. Only 48 percent of the respondents felt that "paying someone to do all the housework" qualified as normal, and only 44 percent agreed that "eating at fine restaurants several times per week" represented normal success. Full-time, live-in childcare was "excessive" for 58 percent of the respondents, while 71 percent disapproved of "having cell phones and/or beepers for kids."[1] The outsourcers we interviewed depart somewhat from these figures. They are more willing (and in some cases more able) than the average person to delegate major aspects of their personal lives so that they can concentrate on a demanding career and spend the rest of their time in carefully selected nonwork activities.

The popularity of outsourcing is easy to understand. Compared to the other rebalancing strategies profiled in this book, outsourcing offers the following advantages:

- Outsourcing can simplify your life to a degree, especially if the alternative is juggling, because it dictates that you off-load certain tasks instead of doing them yourself.
- Compared to alternating, it allows you to stay fully involved in your career. You don't need to step away from intense work commitments in order to get the benefits from outsourcing.
- Unlike techflexing, it doesn't require much investment in or understanding of technology.
- Similar to bundling, outsourcing can force you to clarify your priorities and manage your life accordingly.

Outsourcing is clearly not for everyone, however. To help determine whether outsourcing is a potentially helpful strategy for you, take a moment to fill out the Outsourcing Aptitude Test, after which we'll explore the characteristics of successful outsourcers.

CHARACTERISTICS OF SUCCESSFUL OUTSOURCERS

As suggested by the scoring of the self-test, successful outsourcers don't necessarily possess all of these characteristics—you don't have to score a 10 to get the benefit of this strategy. But you do need to have significant strengths in some of the following areas. If not, outsourcing will probably create more frustration than balance for you.

EXPERIMENTATION (QUESTIONS 1 AND 2)

If you want to outsource, you need to be willing to try new approaches and "think outside the box" when it comes to meeting life's demands. Either by choice or necessity, outsourcers see precious few activities as sacred personal rituals. This, in turn, liberates them from necessary but time-consuming and, for them, unfulfilling tasks.

> "I can't complain about my life," says Chris Watson, "except in one area: the dating scene. Until recently, I had almost no social contact beyond my work colleagues and clients. They're all nice people and good friends, but none of them has potential to be a serious relationship for me."
>
> Chris decided she needed outside help, so she joined Dating for Busy Professionals. The price: $1,000 for nine months. After an interview and profile, the service arranges a date for

Outsourcing Aptitude Test

Place a check mark next to each statement that you believe is true for you.

✓ 1. I enjoy experimenting with new and unusual products, services, and approaches, especially if they promise to save me time and energy.

___ 2. I would describe myself as resourceful and fairly creative in finding the help I need.

✓ 3. I'm a pretty good judge of character; I can usually tell if someone is honest, dependable, and trustworthy before I ask them to do something for me.

✓ 4. I'm a good planner—I think ahead, make arrangements with plenty of lead time, and usually have back-up plans in place in case someone or something falls through.

✓ 5. I'm fortunate to have enough disposable income to buy some services that I would otherwise have to provide myself.

___ 6. Time to do what I want to do is more important to me than money.

___ 7. I have a strong and accessible network of immediate family, neighbors, friends, or church/interest group members with whom I can "trade" services and obligations.

(Continued)

___ 8. I don't feel guilty about relying on the help of people who are close to me, and I know they don't think twice about seeking my assistance with their life demands.

__✓ 9. I have (or could easily generate) a list of things that have to be done but that in no way require my involvement.

__✓ 10. I'm clear about the handful of activities and pursuits that are most worthy of my personal time and attention.

Scoring: Count up the number of check marks you have made. Interpret your scores according to the following rules:

1–3 check marks: Outsourcing probably will not be your most effective strategy for work-life balance.

4–6 check marks: You should at least consider outsourcing as a strategy.

7–10 check marks: Outsourcing is a strategy that may work extremely well for you in your quest to rebalance your life.

lunch, dinner, or entertainment. For security reasons, this first encounter is always in a public place and the two parties are known to each other only by first names, which may be pseudonyms. Follow-up meetings are left up to the two individuals.

But Chris isn't putting all her eggs in one basket. She also belongs to Just for Lunch, a dating service, and subscribes to match.com, a sort of "e-Yenta," which involves extensive e-mail communication before any telephone (much less face-to-face) follow up. So far, only one of the men Chris has met is a serious prospect, but she has no regrets. "I've met some nice guys on my terms and my schedule," she comments, "and I've found out a lot about who I am and what I like."

Chris's efforts to "outsource" part of her social life may be miles outside of your comfort zone, but that's not the point. As a strategy, outsourcing works best for those who'll let go of some traditional notions of "how things are supposed to be done." Notice that Chris hasn't outsourced the process entirely— she doesn't hire someone to go on the dates for her. But she has found a way to get help with the difficult, discouraging, "meat market" aspect of trying to meet interesting men.

Do you love holiday cheer—but you can't stand hanging the Christmas lights? Hire someone to do it. Tired of sending wedding gifts months after the reception because you never get around to it? Subscribe to a gift service. Feeling guilty about feeding your family a staple diet of fast food and ramen noodles instead of home-cooked meals? Organize a neighborhood "chef's co-op." The possibilities are limited only by your discretionary income, your creativity, and your (perhaps not entirely valid) sense of propriety.

MANAGERIAL SKILLS (QUESTIONS 3 AND 4)

Consider the complexities involved in finding capable, trustworthy people to whom you can delegate many of your personal matters. Money cannot buy love—nor can it buy dependability, integrity, and honesty, necessarily. When "staff members" are performing impor-tant functions in your life, reliability and trust are indispensable. Most people who outsource extensively have at least one story of theft, breakage, snooping, drinking from the liquor cabinet, or reck-less endangerment on the part of a hired helper.

In addition to such worries is the sheer complexity of keeping all the comings and goings coordinated. Most outsourcers recognize that managing staff and support personnel can be so demanding that "the staff is managing me," as one person put it. If taken to the extreme, such administrative and scheduling headaches defeat the purpose of outsourcing in the first place. Still, some highly successful professionals see themselves with little choice—and they find a way to make it work.

> Marisa Santos, a finance executive for a Fortune 50 manufacturer in Detroit, hires out everything she can. First on her list is anything to do with her house: repair work, lawn care, snow removal, landscaping, decorating, housecleaning, etc. She does trim her own bushes because she hasn't found anyone she can hire to do it—but she's looking for a gardener. "Life is a constant search for more suppliers," she laughs. While she doesn't have a personal shopper, most of her purchases are made from catalogs or on the Internet "because it's faster."
>
> Then there's the issue of childcare. "This is more complicated than anything I deal with at work," she confesses. Marisa's ex-husband lives nearby, and he takes Laura, their nine-year-old daughter, on Wednesday evenings and every other weekend. The rest of the time, Marisa has one babysitter for Laura from predawn to the time school starts, the same one again from the time school gets out until five o'clock, and a different sitter from five o'clock until she gets home. "If I made a lot more money or married someone with a comparable income," she admits, "my first move would be to hire a full-time, live-in nanny so that Laura didn't have to bounce around all day."
>
> She also has a network of neighbors (mostly the parents of Laura's friends) who help shuttle Laura to after-school activities like Brownies or soccer practice. These same neighbors are Marisa's "emergency fallback" during the day if Marisa can't

get away from work. She tries to reciprocate on weekends by taking the neighbors' kids when she has Laura.

Her ex-husband's mother lives nearby and usually helps out when Laura gets sick and can't go to school or to the sitter. When Laura had the flu and was out of school for ten days, she ended up staying overnight at her grandmother's house a good part of the time. "It was just a lot more convenient for everyone," explains Marisa.

Marisa's advice to would-be outsourcers is unstinting. "You have to be incredibly well organized," she says. "Sometimes people don't show up or don't follow through. There's stress every day wondering if everybody is going to do what they're supposed to do." A bad snowstorm, an attack of the flu, and the carefully orchestrated arrangements can fall apart. "You have to have two or three back-up plans for everything and coordinate an incredible number of resources." Marisa's home calendar not only has all of the events marked that she and Laura are involved in but also two or three reminders to prepare for each event. "You always have to be about five steps ahead of what's going to happen."

This is not a prescription for a stress-free life. But for Marisa, it allows her to balance her two most important priorities: her work (which she loves) and time with Laura. "I do everything I can with Laura, even if it's something mundane like grocery shopping," she says. "Everything else gets outsourced. I want to spend my time and energy making a difference at home and at work. You can't do both and cover all the details, too."

Marisa is perhaps an extreme case, but the principle is undeniable: Outsourcing works best for practitioners who are organized and good at planning. The payoff is more time to devote to those aspects of your life that make a difference.

RESOURCES (QUESTIONS 5 AND 6)

A successful executive, Marisa can afford to purchase all kinds of services. Chris Watson enjoys the same freedom. In fact, many of the outsourcers we interviewed shared this relative affluence, tending toward the upper end of the middle class. Those with less disposable income can and do outsource many activities—a concept we'll explore in the next section of this chapter. But in most cases, outsourcing is not a low-cost strategy.

Of course, money alone does not guarantee happiness. You can probably think of friends and work associates who make plenty of money but never seem to find time to enjoy it. Some of them outsource extensively, only to plow the freed-up time back into their work. For obvious reasons, this doesn't count as a strategy for rebalancing. Central to effective outsourcing is the discipline to *trade money for meaningful nonwork time*. Money is an enabler, but discipline and focus are the real keys to making it work.

The alternative is a vicious cycle: You make a lot of money, which allows you to buy personal services, which in turn allow you to spend even more time making money. To understand how one person broke this cycle, consider the experience of Stacy DeWitt.

> In the aftermath of a painful divorce, Stacy DeWitt, a periodontist in Sacramento, California, found herself turning into a workaholic. She'd met her husband in dental school, where they dreamed of opening a husband-wife dental practice. It became a nightmare, however, when he left her for a younger woman not long after they opened their office.
>
> Stacy dealt with the divorce by throwing herself into her work. She knew that few women dentists had their own practices because of the time demands involved. She was determined to beat the odds. Competent and personable, she soon had a burgeoning and highly profitable practice. For four years,

she did little but work. Her only "vacations" were trips to attend dental conferences, sometimes in exotic locales. She routinely brought paperwork home at night and scheduled patients on weekends.

"It hit me one day that if I was trying to prove I could do it, I had nothing left to prove," she remembers. "I was a huge success—except I didn't have a life."

This epiphany propelled her to action. First, she reworked her schedule so that she sees patients only on Tuesdays, Wednesdays, and Fridays. If a patient cancels, she does not fill the time with paperwork, but takes a short reenergizing nap in a small bedroom set up in her office suite. All financial and administrative matters are handled on Mondays and Thursdays. She no longer allows work to spill over into her evenings. Instead, she volunteers in the community, meditates, reads, travels (much of it still to dental conferences, she admits), spends time with family and friends, and exercises.

To maximize her free time, she buys almost every service available to her. "Paying someone else for basic services makes total economic sense," she says, given the premium she can charge for her hourly services. A housekeeper cleans. A personal assistant does most of her grocery shopping, feeds her dog, and takes it to the veterinarian, allowing Stacy to take it on long walks after work. This same assistant runs miscellaneous errands, purchases gifts, drops off and picks up her dry cleaning, and takes her car in for repairs and maintenance. A gardener tends the plants at both her house and her office.

She considers these people to be part of her staff and focuses on hiring individuals who are positive, competent, and flexible. All of this allows her to take pleasure in the routine tasks she chooses to do herself. "I'm really comfortable with where I am currently," she summarizes.

For Stacy, the willingness to outsource—coupled with the discipline to spend the resulting free time on nonwork activities—has restored a lot of the pleasure to her life and removed much of the drudgery.

A STRONG NETWORK (QUESTIONS 7 AND 8)

What if you're not a periodontist? What if every penny you earn goes toward basic necessities (cold cereal and cable)? Is outsourcing out of reach for you?

Not necessarily. We discovered a thriving approach to outsourcing that is less about resources than resourcefulness. It requires the exchange of social currency, not money. People of all income levels use this technique regularly—and, by most accounts, are happy with the results.

Early in their careers, Jenna and Tony Niccoli lived in a Victorian-era semidetached home in west Philadelphia. Their neighborhood was gentrifying; most of the owners on their street were young professional couples who worked in the greater Philadelphia area, loved the high ceilings and hardwood trim, and couldn't have afforded such architecture in the affluent suburbs. "We could have bought one of those new, cookie-cutter townhomes in King of Prussia or somewhere," recalls Tony, "but we really wanted an older home. This one was in our price range."

Tony was working as a journalist. Jenna was getting her start with a Philadelphia law firm. At the time, their two children were preschoolers. To help buy themselves a few free hours in the evenings after work, they helped organize a neighborhood "Cook's Night Off." Four of the families on their street took turns preparing dinner for the whole group once a month. Not that the neighborhood sat down to eat together—their schedules were too demanding and unpredictable for that. But one night per week, each family could count on a warm, home-cooked meal waiting for them when they got home.

"It wasn't that much harder to prepare a meal for eighteen people than for our family of four," explains Tony, who did most of the cooking. "Larger quantities, obviously, but the prep time was about the same. I decided I'd rather do the work once a month, and get three free evenings in the bargain."

Tony's comment is a classic illustration of "economies of scale," defined as "the decrease in unit manufacturing cost that is due to mass production." That's exactly what makes "Cook's Night Off" workable, and the same principle is at the heart of many outsourcing-on-a-shoestring techniques. For example, a number of student spouses and working parents in Berkeley, California, have organized a babysitting exchange. Participating parents earn coupons by tending other people's kids, an activity that doesn't take any more time (though quite a bit more patience and energy) than tending their own. They can then redeem the coupons when they need an hour, a morning, or a day of time away from their own children.

Perhaps the most widespread approach to budget-minded outsourcing is the use of one's extended family (usually siblings or parents) as service providers. There's nothing new about this practice—grandparents, aunts, and uncles have supplied childcare for thousands of years. For some families, it's the perfect solution.

Dillon and Eileen Johnson are a moderate-income couple with three children in a small Utah town. Dillon teaches at a junior high school; Eileen is a social worker. Dillon's mother, Kate, takes care of the couple's children each week. "My husband

and I don't have any money to help our kids get ahead," says Kate, "but we can give them our time. We always turn out to help landscape, paint, and wallpaper. As for the babysitting," she adds, "I don't want anyone outside the family raising my grandchildren." Such a willing and trusted caregiver is a godsend for the Johnsons, allowing them to pursue their chosen careers and have a rich family life.

The consistent thread in all of these examples is the use of social ties—family, friends, neighbors, or others—to help with life's demands. A strong network is what makes it possible.

FOCUS (QUESTIONS 9 AND 10)

As mentioned earlier, outsourcing, if you're not careful, can be a highly effective strategy for work-life *imbalance:* hire out your household duties, delegate your distractions, and focus almost exclusively on your job. Yet even if you take the time gained by outsourcing and dedicate it to your home life, there's no guarantee you'll feel more balanced. The trick is to figure out which aspects of your nonwork life will provide you with the greatest sense of well-being, then focus your discretionary time and energy on those aspects.

This might sound simple, but it's not. Life is filled with distractions; for each one that we outsource, there are dozens of others lined up, competing for our attention. Imagine the folly of hiring out your weekly yard work, then allocating the resulting hour or two of time to watching *Seinfeld* reruns or to perusing the week's accumulation of mail-order catalogs. Unless such activities honestly charge your batteries, you're probably buying yourself leisure without balance.

Clarity, therefore, is key—clarity about your values and the most satisfying ways to spend the increments of time gained by outsourcing.

Joel Klein, an Internet executive in his late forties, lives in Short Hills, New Jersey, with his wife, Becca, and their two sons, Josh and Aaron. Becca has a graduate degree in sociology but decided early to be a full-time mom. On top of that, she is extremely involved (typically in leadership positions) in the PTA, League of Women Voters, projects for senior citizens, and other ad hoc community committees.

With both parents absorbed in their work, they've chosen to outsource many routine aspects of their lives and to get help with providing educational experiences for their sons. Josh, age 17, takes fencing lessons on Mondays and Wednesdays and participates in tournaments twice a month. He also runs cross-country. Fourteen-year-old Aaron sees a math tutor on Tuesdays, works with a trainer on Thursdays, and—like his older brother—is a talented athlete, deeply involved in two varsity sports.

Over the years, Joel and Becca have counted on picking up dinner most evenings from local neighborhood restaurants. They depend on weekly help in housecleaning and laundry. A gardener takes care of yard work, although Becca insists on tending the flower garden herself. "We have a family of four and a staff of eight," quips Joel. Yet having others perform these services allows Becca and him time to invest in one of their priority activities: the luxury to "just spend time" with their sons.

"We feel it's very important to eat together," says Joel. "Family conversation over dinner is something we zealously protect—but it's not important who prepares the food." The parents scrupulously attend the boys' fencing and lacrosse matches whenever possible. "We won't miss these events," Joel insists. "In fact, I'll schedule business around the games." They also find other ways to squeeze balance out of their busy lives, primarily by bundling. For example, Joel drives Josh to a

Saturday morning course at Columbia University so that they can have the commute for connecting time, then visits his brother and family, who live nearby, while Josh is in class. They consciously promote family interactions, often piggybacking on Joel's business travel to have family vacations in interesting places.

Joel gives a decisive overview of their priorities when he says, "Becca and I decided early on that providing a good education and enriched extracurricular activities, plus lots of hang time, was the bottom line for success in our family. If you asked the boys, they might say that we should do less as a family; after all, they're teenagers. But I think they'd also say that we're close, and that their mother and I know them well and spend lots of time interacting with them."

Outsourcing, says Joel, is a way to support these objectives and still maintain busy and accomplished professional lives—"but we only outsource the stuff that doesn't add value to our family," he insists.

Chris Watson, mentioned earlier, outsources her food and transportation requirements so that she can spend a lot of time with the youth group at her church. Stacy Dewitt buys time for "self-care" (exercise, reading, and naps) by delegating a lot of drudgery to her "staff." Marisa Santos manages to be an active, involved single mom by hiring others to do a lot of her home and yard care. For each of these busy people, outsourcing isn't mere avoidance of unpleasant duties; each of them could complete the sentence, "I'm outsourcing certain activities so that I can spend more time on . . ." with a personally meaningful answer.

Deciding what "adds value" to your life is intensely personal and inescapably subjective. What is for one person a menial task is for another a labor of love. According to an old Spanish saying, *Sobre gustos, no hay nada escrito*—roughly translated, "There's no official guidebook regarding preferences." But outsourcing works best when the balance seeker knows what experiences are indispensable and which can be delegated.

Granted, it's not always easy to keep the priorities clear. Abandoned options sometimes have a way of coming back, bringing with them a freight of regret. Different life stages bring different demands. As one editorial writer mused, "The problem with outsourcing your life is that you lose touch with certain emotional and sensual realities. It's psychologically healthy to keep in touch with your living environment (e.g., clean house). What if you never walk the dog or pick out a present for Mom?"[2]

Chris Watson, reflecting on a question about the downside of her outsourced life, commented, "When I started out, I thought my job and the money it brought was the ticket to learning, excitement, and freedom. Now I'm thirty years old. I feel beat up by all the travel, and I don't have enough time for my personal life. I can't cook or sew on a button. I really think I've missed out on some basic elements of living."

Stacy DeWitt, though happy with the balance she has achieved in her periodontal practice, still has unfinished business about her divorce. "My ex-husband was a creep and left me for a younger woman," she states, "but how much did my busy life contribute to this relationship failure?"

Joel and Becca Klein underwent a separation about fifteen years ago. Like many couples, they weren't communicating well and needed to find a way to renew their marriage. "But," says Joel, "when I finally started to listen to what Becca was really saying— that I was way out of balance—I decided to change. That's when I began taking family time much more seriously and aggressively outsourcing the marginal stuff." Fortunately, Joel earns a substantial income and could afford such services. His visible commitment to the family helped rejuvenate a marriage now in its thirtieth year.

WEIGHING THE TRADE-OFFS

These last observations from Chris, Stacy, and Joel highlight some of the trade-offs inherent in outsourcing. As mentioned repeatedly in this book, there's no such thing as a "perfect" approach to rebalancing your life. At least, we haven't found one yet. While outsourcing is a viable and valuable technique, it helps if you are utterly realistic about its potential stress points.

TIME VERSUS MONEY

"We are engulfed in a world of privatized care where many of us are working just to be cared for," warns Arlie Hochschild, a sociologist at U.C. Berkeley. She identifies middle-class families as particularly vulnerable to getting caught in a vicious cycle: "They move to expensive homes and apartments, install expensive security systems because they are away so much, outsource everything, escape, and essentially, are working longer hours to make up the economic difference."[3]

In short, it takes money to buy these goods and services, but earning money takes time. Where is the boundary between enough and too much? At what point does the expense of outsourcing defeat its own purpose?

TIME VERSUS ENERGY

As Marisa Santos articulated so clearly, outsourcing creates a network of dependency on (usually) hired hands. It takes enormous energy to arrange everything, create back-up plans, and deal with last-minute changes. Nonmonetary outsourcing requires extra effort, too. Babysitting eight kids may not take more time than tending your own, but it definitely requires more energy. If your outsourcing efforts yield a bit of free time, but you're too tired to enjoy it, what's the point?

The average U.S. household spends 45 percent of its disposable income on services.[4] That figure is probably low for serious outsourcers. Beyond the money, however, are the transaction costs of maintaining all those outsourcing relationships. As University of Arizona researcher Barbara Gutek points out, the more personal the service, the more time and energy consuming the relationship. When you outsource, you become an employer, but you have to adjust to your employees' schedules, find a substitute or do the job yourself when the employee is unavailable (for example, sick, on vacation, on jury duty), and spend an enormous amount of time searching for the "right" employee in the first place. She cautions busy professionals to recognize the time drain, as well as the advantages, built into outsourcing relationships.[5]

AUTONOMY VERSUS INTERDEPENDENCE

Professor Gutek's warning points to another trade-off: the loss of independence. Outsourcing is pretty much the opposite of self-sufficiency. Your life can become a complex system of "entangling alliances," actually jeopardizing the freedom you sought in the first place.

Outsourcers have to balance the benefits of delegating some of their chores against the disadvantage of potential dependence on, or even exploitation by, their "staff." When service providers are, in Stacy DeWitt's words, "positive, competent, and flexible," it's an ideal situation. But few situations are—or remain—ideal for long. Service providers quit, get married, have babies, move, get sick, or want different work. Not even above-market wages can guarantee loyalty and commitment.

PERSONAL INVOLVEMENT VERSUS LETTING GO

"No matter how much I'm willing to pay," lamented an office manager and mother of three, "I can't find anyone who will clean a toilet the way I want it done." It should be noted that her personal technique includes scrubbing the toilet bowl with an Ajax-laden toothbrush, but we all have certain quirks that we hold dear. Outsourcing often means settling for a level of quality or attentiveness well below what we would do ourselves. One of our colleagues stated it more succinctly, if more cynically. "Outsourcers," he said, "spend all of their time on two things: finding people to do stuff and then fixing what they do."

Probably the area of greatest anxiety for parents is outsourcing some aspects of childcare. It takes only a few horrifying tales from less-than-exemplary day-care centers for parents to develop a wariness bordering on paranoia. In response, growing numbers of day-care centers in the United States now offer Webcam-based systems that let working parents monitor their children's care from pop-up windows on their office computers. Other Webcam systems allow you to view what's going on at home from your computer desktop. That's impressive technology, certainly, but such "virtual" options fall woefully short of the responsiveness and interaction you could provide "live."

This trade-off has additional implications for families when it comes to reinforcing a family work ethic and communicating values. Most of the parents we interviewed agreed that it's important to work side by side with their children, teaching them basic survival skills such as cooking, cleaning, and repairing things, all the while showing them that such tasks are valuable contributions to a happy family life. But busy families are sorely and understandably tempted to forego such menial chores in favor of recreational, cultural, or educational activities. You can pay a neighborhood teen to mow your lawn, but you'd never hire someone to take your daughter to the ballet, would you?

Jessica De Groot, a work-life consultant, has pondered, "Is everyone working, and leaving the family side of 'work and family' to hired hands? If so, what's the implication?"[6] This is far from an abstract question for Joel Klein. "Becca and I are very involved in all that constitutes the boys' extended life," he says, "but we haven't done that much physical labor together as a family. I just hope we have it right."

SUMMARY

Outsourcing—the process of delegating some of life's demands to others—is one of the most common strategies for rebalancing work and nonwork demands. In fact, we all do it to some degree. Those who are most successful at it are willing to

- Try new ways of doing things

- Invest time and energy in planning and managing service providers

- Trade money for time

- Involve their network of social support

- Rigorously clarify their priorities and invest their saved time in activities that yield the greatest sense of well-being in their lives

While many of the examples in this chapter are extreme cases, outsourcing is not an "all-or-nothing" strategy. The majority of outsourcers notice a marked improvement in their quality of life simply by identifying one or two menial activities that they can hire out.

Ideas for Small-Scale Outsourcing

- Take advantage of gift wrapping or delivery services when you buy items on-line or through a catalog.

- Pick up stir-fry-in-a-bag and other convenience foods at the grocery store.

- Hire someone to do the household chore you most dislike.

- Stop and get a shoe shine next time you're in an airport or train station.

- Organize a carpool—for yourself or for your busiest children.

- Try to expand the services you buy from a single provider. For example, if you hire a lawn service, see if they will also weed your flower beds or hang Christmas lights.

5

Bundling

CAMILLE HARRELLS, a health care consultant, settles her four-year-old, Dylan, into the middle seat as Cathy, Dylan's nanny, hoists her carry-on bag into the overhead bin and takes the aisle seat. Camille will spend the next two days with a client in Chicago, while Dylan and Cathy see the sights of the city. In the evenings, Camille will join them for dinner at a Pakistani restaurant (something that isn't available in their hometown of Omaha) and watch an IMAX film on dinosaurs, Dylan's latest passion.

This type of excursion is a regular ritual for Camille and her two preschoolers. She originally had doubts about taking a travel-intensive job. When her new employer approved taking the nanny and the children along on business trips, she started to see a silver lining. Camille and her husband, David, a professor, chose to live in Omaha because of the low crime rates, close-knit neighborhoods, and an overall wholesome environment. They worried, though, about what the kids might be missing.

"We want them to experience a lot of different cultures and people," says Camille, "and traveling with me on business gives them the best of both worlds. It also makes being on the road a lot less lonely for me."

Combining corporate travel with family togetherness isn't easy. "And it's definitely not cheap," Camille adds. "That obviously limits the frequency of our outings. Clients pay for my travel expenses, but the other two plane tickets and extra hotel and meal charges come out of my pocket, and that doesn't even account for the nanny's salary." Extra details add to the stress of a routine business trip: finding a hotel that has two-room suites or hoping the rental car company remembers the car seat. "But as my kids grow up, we'll have great memories of all of our adventures together. And hopefully it will help them realize all of the options that are available as they choose what they want to do with their lives."

Camille is proficient at packing multiple purposes into a single event or activity—a rebalancing strategy we call bundling. She's quick to point out that bundling is not just for the business traveler. "I think about it in everything I do. For example, I'm meeting a friend for lunch today. When we were deciding where to eat, I thought about the rest of my to-do list. I want to pick up some items at the health food store, which is near our mortgage company where I need to drop off some documents. I'm also trying to eat more vegetables and less meat. So lunch at the vegetarian café next to the health food store (and across the street from the mortgage company) seemed like the logical choice."

MULTIPURPOSING, NOT MULTITASKING

As a coping mechanism, bundling is ages old. Before the industrial revolution, work life, home life, and community life were all one life. Most families earned their living from the same activities that were central to keeping house—farming or home-based craftsmanship. Merchants lived above or near their stores. "Working at home" could have meant simply taking a hot bath or washing the dishes—onerous chores when you haul and heat your own water. Such a labor-intensive lifestyle left little time for meeting social needs. As a result, our forebears looked for ways to fulfill both purposes with a single activity. Need a barn built? Gather the neighbors and host a potluck party at the same time. Need more blankets for winter? Invite the women to a quilting bee, and in the bargain get a support group for comparing notes on marriage, child rearing, and farm/home management.

As the industrial revolution developed, more and more domains of daily life were cordoned off from each other. Fathers left home to work elsewhere; many mothers have recently joined them. People's lives grew out of synch with the lives of their neighbors as suburban life replaced farm life and city life. Modern conveniences fostered self-reliance and eliminated the motivation to make a friend of a neighbor while asking for a helping hand. Increasingly diverse communities and family compositions mean that people may have less in common with their neighbors in the first place.

Schedules have become more frenetic for both adults and children, and most families are finding it more and more difficult to spend time at home together, much less attend the community activities that predominated calendars a century or more ago. This increasing fragmentation can contribute to lives that feel busy but incomplete, as average citizens lose their ability and need to call on the community for help and social support.

Today, many find they must head in various directions to earn a living, maintain relationships with family and friends, and pursue personal development. In less complicated eras, those needs were met under a single roof.

Kevin Childers and his wife, Nancy, have taken dramatic steps to counterbalance the breakup of traditional communities by building their own. Both lead very busy lives. Kevin is an engineer for a global chemicals company, and Nancy homeschools their five children. By bundling, they manage to maintain a network of close family friends who share common interests and values.

"We've made a lot of close friends through the local home schooling network, as well as with a number of people in our congregation at church," Kevin notes. "The things we do for social activities might not appeal to most people, but to us, they're fun. Most of them involve some type of work. For instance, when someone in our group of friends is doing a major home improvement project, we involve the whole family and help them out. Our older daughters are teenagers, so they either help with the work we're doing or play games with the younger kids. When the work is finished, we order a pizza and have a meal together."

Given their long list of daily demands, the Childers would probably forego this type of socializing if they couldn't accomplish something else at the same time. "Most of our friends are as busy as we are," Kevin explains. "If we don't find ways to combine work and fun, the fun is undoubtedly what would get left out."

Bundling in some ways resembles juggling. Both help the balancer accomplish multiple goals in a limited amount of time. Bundling is much more than a hyper-thyroid approach to multitasking, however. In some ways, it's the opposite. The essence of bundling is to do fewer activities, but to pack more meaning into each one of them—more *multipurposing* than multitasking.

For example, Camille Harrells will look at an upcoming business trip—something she will be doing in any case—and tweak it a bit so that it meets more than one need. She recently spotted a week in her work schedule in which she'd be shuttling between Detroit and Manhattan. Her husband's parents live in upstate New York, roughly midway between her two destinations. "My in-laws hadn't seen the kids in over a year," she said, "and David was also eager to spend some time with his mom and dad. I had heard of a spa resort in upstate New York that I wanted to try, and the trip happened to be the same week as my birthday—in June, just after David turned in grades for his spring classes. It didn't take too much extra work to arrange for David and the children to spend time with David's parents while I was working in the same region. Then David and I spent the weekend at the spa, while the kids got some time alone with their grandparents. It also gave us a great childcare option while we went off for a romantic weekend together. And it actually ended up being cheaper than a normal vacation would have been for our family, because my ticket was paid for by my client—with the added bonus for them of a Saturday-night-stay fare."

If Camille were a juggler, she might have tried to fit more activities in—perhaps racing back to Omaha in between the New York and Michigan trips—which would have accomplished less and caused much more physical and emotional wear and tear. Because of its paradoxical emphasis on both simplifying and doing more, bundling is much more sustainable than juggling as a long-term strategy. The motto of people who use this strategy extensively might be Doing More with Less. They find ways to milk more meaning out of a single experience, rather than adding more items to the agenda.

We definitely identified a bundling "type" and we can pinpoint characteristic skills that make bundling easier. This strategy is realistically available to almost anyone, however, and there is much to be learned from serious bundlers. In comparison to the other strategies covered in this book, bundling offers the following advantages.

LOW COST

Unlike outsourcing, alternating, or techflexing, bundling is a financial bargain. You don't have to earn more to get more mileage out of a single experience. In fact, in many of the examples we heard in our interviews, bundling saved both money and time.

MULTIPURPOSING

Bundlers often are able to continue activities that they would otherwise have to sacrifice at various life stages. Scott Hillard, who owns a publishing firm, has three priorities outside of work: spending time outdoors, doing things with his teenage sons, and "giving back" through community service. "If I try to do all three separately, they either don't get done, or don't get done as well as I'd like them to." Scott's answer is to volunteer as the leader of his sons' scout troop. "I get to know the kids and their friends in a way that I wouldn't if they were just hanging around the house," he says, "and I also get to go camping—something I'd probably have to give up at this point in my life if I couldn't combine it with other things."

ENRICHED EXPERIENCES

Bundling two or more activities together can actually enrich one experience in unexpected ways. One clergyman makes a habit of looking for ways to double up activities on the church calendar— which allows him to fit more events into his schedule. When he noticed that the youth group had a service project planned for the same week that the seniors had scheduled a dinner party, he suggested combining them. The result was that the youth served dinner for the seniors and got to know parish members near their grandparents' age—far outside their usual social circle. Intergenerational friendships formed that wouldn't have developed from the two activities alone.

EMOTIONAL ADVANTAGES

In comparison to juggling, bundling is emotionally easier. Focusing on fewer activities saves wear and tear, conserving energy to enjoy each experience more. Bundlers also make choices about what they *won't do,* reducing the guilt and frustration about not being able to do it all. Because bundling focuses on integrating people and ideas across boundaries, it can also provide a more holistic and sustainable approach to managing multiple priorities.

SMALL WINS

Although the people we interviewed use bundling extensively, it's an ideal add-on strategy. Just bundling two activities into one frees up time and doesn't require any major lifestyle changes or personality traits.

The following self-assessment provides an overview of the key capabilities or attitudes needed to make bundling work for you.

CHARACTERISTICS OF SUCCESSFUL BUNDLERS

A WILLINGNESS TO INTEGRATE AND ERASE OR IGNORE TRADITIONAL BOUNDARIES (QUESTIONS I AND 2)

Bundlers bring things together. They question traditional assumptions about how activities and relationships should be grouped. When they see a problem, they wonder how they might "integrate" around it. When Camille Harrells found herself tempted to turn down an exciting and rewarding job offer, she started thinking about how she could reframe her priorities. That reevaluation made the glaring downside of the opportunity not just tolerable but modestly beneficial.

In most cases, this doesn't mean challenging societal taboos or ruffling feathers. Toting one's children along on a business trip is not exactly conventional, but it's not shocking, either. It takes more work than making the trip alone, but also pays more dividends. In most cases, a willingness to think creatively about how to enrich an experience or marshal resources dramatically increases the effectiveness of an activity without increasing the amount of time spent.

Bundling Aptitude Test

Place a check mark next to each statement that you believe is true of you.

_____ 1. I like combining both relationships and activities from the various domains of my life. For example, I'm comfortable combining personal pursuits with work responsibilities.

_____ 2. I'm comfortable combining activities and relationships in ways that might seem unconventional to most people. I think that real benefits come from having a minimum of boundaries in my life.

✓ 3. I'm good at planning and organizing. I can manage multiple priorities simultaneously.

_____ 4. I manage my time effectively. I generally avoid underestimating the amount of time a particular activity will require.

✓ 5. I like creating structure for myself and others. I believe that I can get more things done when I lay out all the details ahead of time.

_____ 6. I maintain a broad net of reciprocal relationships in both my personal and professional lives.

_____ 7. I'm good at keeping a variety of people "in the loop"; I communicate often and extensively with those in my personal and professional networks.

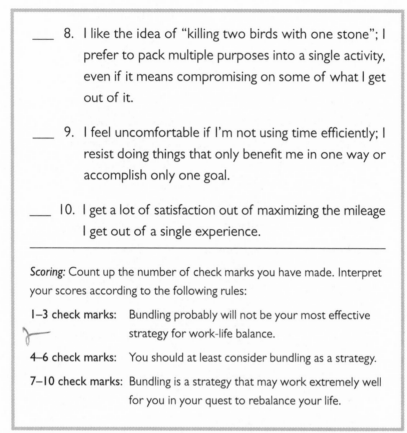

___ 8. I like the idea of "killing two birds with one stone"; I prefer to pack multiple purposes into a single activity, even if it means compromising on some of what I get out of it.

___ 9. I feel uncomfortable if I'm not using time efficiently; I resist doing things that only benefit me in one way or accomplish only one goal.

___ 10. I get a lot of satisfaction out of maximizing the mileage I get out of a single experience.

Scoring: Count up the number of check marks you have made. Interpret your scores according to the following rules:

1–3 check marks: Bundling probably will not be your most effective strategy for work-life balance.

4–6 check marks: You should at least consider bundling as a strategy.

7–10 check marks: Bundling is a strategy that may work extremely well for you in your quest to rebalance your life.

In her first year of teaching middle school French, Diane Anderson hosted a medieval feast for her advanced French students and cast them in an accompanying medieval play. The original purpose of the event was simple enough—to share her passion for medieval history with her eighth-grade students. Over time, Diane began finding additional purposes for the feast. She extended it to include all her French classes, with coveted roles in the feast and play used as rewards for hard-working students. Later, the feast expanded to include all interested students in the school—and their parents. She saw she could draw in shy or struggling kids. Giving them a role at the feast provided them with a way to create friendships and build confidence.

Although preparing the feast was an easy task in the early years, when it grew into multiple feasts scheduled over a period of a week, Diane needed help. Because there were no medieval caterers in the local community and because she was working on a public school budget, Diane began involving family and friends in the meal preparation. Neighbors, colleagues from other schools, family members, and former students and their parents pitched in to help with the kitchen work and cleanup. Over time, this diverse group of Diane's friends—who in everyday life probably would never have met—evolved into a close community. Putting on the feast was a monumental task for Diane, but it gave her a way to build an annual tradition for the school and spend time with a vast array of friends and colleagues. "The feast never would have grown if it weren't for Diane's creativity about how to get people involved," said her principal. "Most people wouldn't have thought beyond the boundaries of the original classroom of advanced French students."

When Diane left the school after eighteen years, the objectives accomplished by the feast—drawing in less-involved students, rewarding outstanding accomplishment, teaching medieval history, and more—were divided among seven different teachers. After one year of sincere efforts, the principal felt that the group of teachers combined hadn't accomplished as much as Diane had with a single event. "These teachers have honestly tried," he said. "I think they've fallen short because they worked individually to meet each objective independently. We had too many different systems, processes, and events. It got to be too complicated and diffused everyone's focus. It was just too much work for both the teachers and the students."

Bundling occasionally involves integrating activities with a long history of separation. A recent *Fortune* magazine cover story reported on a growing trend to combine worship and business.[1] The article featured organizations such as the Chicago-based Business Leaders for Excellence, Ethics, and Justice (BLEEJ), a group of Catholic executives who use their faith to improve the business environment. "I like to think of us as anti-Dilberts," explains Gregory Pearce, cofounder of BLEEJ and author of a book called *Spirituality@Work*. According to the article, people of faith aren't just looking for ways to fit church attendance into their busy schedules or use business contacts to proselytize their faith. Rather, they are part of a growing movement to improve the business environment by integrating spiritual concepts into everyday business life.

"Most of us spend so much time working, it would be a shame if we couldn't find God there," says Pearce. "There is a creative energy in work that is somehow tied to God's creative energy. If we can understand that connection, perhaps we can use it to transform the workplace into something remarkable." The group promotes a range of tactics to bundle work and spiritual life—from sponsoring interdenominational seminars and conferences to reevaluating company ethics policies to reducing the dissonance between personal beliefs and corporate practices. "The goal here isn't to rally the troops behind yet another office blood drive," he says. "It's to make the workplace a more ethical and humane arena, one where believers and nonbelievers alike can find fulfillment."[2]

Of course, attempting to bridge the gap between the cubicle and the cathedral has raised corporate hackles. Given the amount of wrong done in God's name over the ages and the implications for freedom of religion in a power-laden environment, the taboo against mixing commerce with faith is not without foundation. Many people are made equally uncomfortable by growing efforts by some faiths to appeal to corporate citizens, such as hiring former executives or investment bankers to lead spiritual retreats. The Reverend

Dr. Thomas K. Tewell, senior pastor of the Fifth Avenue Presbyterian Church in New York City, uses his Faith@Work lecture series to encourage business people to become "points of distribution" for God's love or to be "channels in the divine economy."

For those comfortable with these unconventional metaphors, such integration translates spiritual concepts into terminology that is familiar and easy to grasp. In fact, it may enhance both experiences—making faith less compartmentalized and the corporate world more sensitive. For others, erasing the boundaries between two sectors traditionally seen as incompatible, or even antithetical, is distasteful and unappealing; they prefer to keep their faith in one box and their professional life in another. The key point is that a willingness to experiment with bundling the two, even in the face of raised eyebrows, may allow more time for both business and spiritual pursuits.

PLANNING AND ORGANIZING (QUESTIONS 3 THROUGH 5)

All of the bundlers we interviewed agreed that logistics were a challenge. Picture the Childers family's weekly planning sessions: "Every Sunday night we all sit down with a big white board. We list everything that needs to be done during the week—activities, errands, and so on. We chart out the events that are scheduled for a specific day and time and then plot out where they are geographically in the community. Then we fill in the activities that can be done anytime according to when someone will be in the same area at the right time of day. Our oldest daughter has her driver's license. She sometimes gets annoyed if we ask her to go on a lot of extra errands for us—realistically, she's as busy as my wife and I are and doesn't have a lot of free time. But if she can pick up something at the store or drop off or pick up one of the younger kids on her way to or from something that she needs to do anyway, she's more than happy to help us out."

The Childers are firm believers in this "dispatch" approach to planning. When they had to miss a few Sunday night planning sessions to attend a child's baseball games, their lives began to go downhill. "We haven't been able to fit nearly as much in—everything seems to take much, much more time. It's dramatically increased the stress level in our family."

Kelly Baker, an IT consultant in Northern California, is working on a social science degree through the University of Washington's on-line program, where she's also involved in student government. Trying to balance those commitments—while fitting in time with her husband, two dogs, and a large circle of friends—requires a lot of forethought.

"In a lot of ways, it's just thinking ahead about what you can double up," she says. "I'll finish my degree the same year that my husband and I celebrate our tenth wedding anniversary. We're planning one big vacation that will celebrate both. On an everyday basis, if I need to meet with someone at work, I often plan it over lunch—since I need to eat anyway. Or if I need to go into San Francisco, I think about how many things I can accomplish with one trip. If I go in to the city for a dentist appointment, I might also be able to meet with a client, do some shopping, or pick up some information for one of my school projects."

Kelly admits that sometimes her plans go awry and her schedule gets thrown off kilter. "When I took the Balance Strategies Profile (see chapter 9), I scored highest on bundling and a close second on juggling. I always try to accomplish many objectives at once as a first choice. When the plan falls apart—say, if someone I really want to stay in touch with can't make it to a movie or concert that I've already bought tickets for—I resort to juggling. In this case, I'd probably do whatever I had planned, plus find another time to get together with the friend who couldn't make it—which means twice as much activity for the same outcome. Juggling definitely increases my stress level; it's much harder than bundling."

Planning also means effective time management, which goes beyond effective use of a day planner or Palm Pilot. In contrast to her own bundling expertise, Kelly points out that her sister has repeatedly attempted to bundle, with most of her efforts ending in failure. "She plans ahead, but then her schedule falls apart because she underestimates the amount of time that something will take. If she's planned to run five errands in one trip and has a limited amount of time, one item on her list might end up taking twice as long as she thought it would. Then she has to make at least one more trip because she runs out of time. So she ends up not saving much time, even after all that planning."

In many cases, time management is a critical issue simply because of the number of things that bundlers are trying to accomplish. "When I was an undergraduate, I was a full-time student, in addition to working two jobs," says Tina Sosa, a recruiter for a Seattle high-tech company. "I worked forty hours a week as a guest services clerk in a popular business hotel. I also worked twenty hours a week in the business school's administrative office. I needed the income from both jobs to get through school, but the big time commitment could have made it impossible to succeed. So I went out of my way to find jobs that would accomplish additional goals." At the hotel, things were fairly quiet after 8:00 P.M. because most of the guests were checked in. By working all night, she had plenty of time to study, without the distractions of roommates or social opportunities that might have tempted her at home. The business school job also was multipurpose: "I built great relationships with other business students that are still part of my network ten years later. Rubbing shoulders with the faculty also gave me a chance for informal learning that I wouldn't have had otherwise, given the amount of time I spent working."

Despite the clear emphasis on planning and structure reflected in every bundling interview, the stories we heard made it clear that the tendency to structure every activity also needs to be tempered with a measure of flexibility. "Bundling extensively is like working on several levels at once," Kelly Baker told us. "When one level doesn't work out the way you thought it would, you have to be willing to adjust the other levels accordingly." Tina Sosa described the same need in a different way. "Bundling is like putting together a giant puzzle. A change in one piece affects everything else. You have to be able to adapt."

NETWORKING AND COMMUNICATION (QUESTIONS 6 AND 7)

Bundlers are good at staying in touch. Those we talked to consistently look for opportunities to involve friends and family in whatever they do. Many hands make light work, of course, but bringing friends along also makes an experience more emotionally satisfying. Diane Anderson's gigantic medieval feast tapped her friends' goodwill but gave all of them an excuse to spend time with each other. Her ability to make it fun for the volunteers (as well as the kids) helped them look forward to the annual event, rather than seeing it as a dreaded burden.

Bundlers know that this quid pro quo is essential. Kevin and Nancy Childers help their friends, knowing they'll receive in kind when they face an emergency or undertake a major project—especially if they build some entertainment or food into the agenda. Kelly Baker maintains her web of relationships not only because the friendships are satisfying in and of themselves but also as a way to create a safety net for when her plans hit a snag. "I've built up enough credits with the people I'm close to, or who I work with closely, that I know I can be late occasionally, or ask them to help me at the last minute, without damaging our friendship."

Bundling family and friends into one's exercise, hobbies, or home improvement doesn't just happen. It takes effort. Sandra Gammon, a training coordinator who lives in Pennsylvania, spent several years at home when her children were young. "I looked at being a mother as my full-time job during that time and planned regular activities that I thought would be fun and meaningful for the kids—like going to the zoo, or to a ballgame, or to the local history museum," she remembers. "I usually invited a couple of my friends to bring their children along. If I had waited for them to call me, nothing ever would have happened. Even though tracking them down and making all the arrangements took more work than just going on my own, it almost always made the experience better. I got to spend time with my friends, and really enjoyed being able to talk to a grown up. My kids got to make friends with children that they wouldn't have known otherwise, and they also got to know my friends. Some of those relationships continue now that they are adults."

A PASSION FOR EFFICIENCY (QUESTIONS 8 THROUGH 10)

If efficiency wasn't the highest priority for the bundlers we interviewed, it was always near the top of their list. "I would rather pay the late fee on videos than make a special trip just to return them on time," says Tina Sosa, the Seattle recruiter. "If I can't think of another errand that takes me to the same part of town, my time is worth more than the couple of dollars it costs me to take them back a day late." When Kevin Childers tried to pick up a prescription at the drugstore on his way home from his son's baseball game, he found the doors locked. "It really bothered me that the store was closed by the time we got there. We needed the medicine—so I had to go back when the store was open. It took almost an hour out of my Sunday afternoon, and I didn't accomplish anything else while I was out."

Like seasoned business travelers who learn to minimize baggage by packing multipurpose clothes, bundlers look for efficiencies in their to-do lists. "It's hard for me to justify doing something if it's only going to accomplish one goal," says Camille Harrels. Her brother, a professional percussionist based in Cincinnati, was giving a solo performance as the culmination of his graduate studies. "I really wanted to go to the concert," Camille reasons, "but it was hard to justify going just for that. So I tried to arrange some work in the same trip. I thought one of my clients in New Jersey might need me there that week, and it would be easy to stop in Cincinnati on the way. I also thought about the fact that both of my parents would be attending the concert. Maybe we could plan a family vacation around it and take the kids."

This kind of thinking is second nature to most bundlers. In fact, the desire for efficiency may lead to some major life restructuring.

Lyle Hanna was working as a Louisville-based human resources consultant with William M. Mercer Company. His passion outside of work, however, was helping Habitat for Humanity build homes worldwide for people who otherwise couldn't afford them. As chair of Habitat's global committee, Lyle was organizing projects in sixty-eight countries and building relationships with business executives around the world in order to secure local support for the charitable projects. He spent all of his vacations in remote spots of the world—from Ghana to Guatemala—pounding nails and laying shingles. Lyle's weekday job at Mercer was enjoyable, although the scope seemed small in comparison to his volunteer job. His work territory was all within easy driving distance of his home—the loop from Louisville to Cincinnati to Lexington.

As Lyle wrapped up a vacation spent with one hundred volunteers building three homes for Maori families in New Zealand, he had an epiphany. When he returned to the United States, he proposed a new role for himself at Mercer that would enable him to build Mercer's business worldwide, using his broad network of executive relationships. At the same time, it would allow him to leverage his business trips to accomplish significantly more for Habitat for Humanity. He insists that Mercer always comes first, recalling a canceled Habitat trip to Katmandu that allowed him to meet with an important client in Kentucky. Ironically enough, he first met the client because they serve together on the Habitat for Humanity board.

In his new global business development role, Lyle meets with the leaders of Mercer affiliates worldwide. At the same time, he meets with local Habitat for Humanity leaders and moves projects forward at a faster rate than he could using only his vacation time and the resources of a nonprofit organization.[3]

In Lyle Hanna's situation, real efficiency wasn't possible without a major overhaul to align his work and nonwork priorities. His example is extreme, but smaller efficiencies may be gained from realigning priorities. For example, Kevin Childers noticed that the teenagers at his church, including his daughter, were always headed in a different direction from the rest of the family when it came to activities. He helped redesign the youth group so that it included other family members on occasion. Instead of having game nights just for the teens, they began asking parents of the youth to plan activities in their homes. They also planned service activities such as visiting nursing homes or repairing the homes of those in need and then involved parents in the activities as well.

WEIGHING THE TRADE-OFFS

Bundling is one of the easiest strategies to use if you're willing to make some trade-offs:

STRUCTURE VERSUS SPONTANEITY

Bundling leans heavily on structure, often to the exclusion of spontaneity. "Sometimes I think it's sad that our lives have become so heavily planned," says Sandra Gammon, the Pennsylvania training coordinator. "I wonder what I miss out on because I can't take advantage of many last minute opportunities."

Taken to an extreme, the structure involved in bundling may actually create additional stress when plans don't work out. Tina Sosa has a daily walk built into her schedule that accomplishes several purposes: exercise, enjoyment of the wooded area near her home, and walking her two dogs. When the two dogs were puppies, however, she found that having to take care of them definitely cramped her style. "I couldn't go for my walk until my husband got home from work, because the puppies were too small to take along and I didn't want to leave them alone after being at work all day. I ended up feeling really frustrated because I had to do the two things sequentially instead of simultaneously; it felt like a real waste of time."

Another frustration for those who bundle extensively is a feeling of regret when they could have bundled and didn't, or when they could have combined even more purposes into an activity. When Camille Harrells traveled to Orlando for business, she took an afternoon to visit Universal Studios but regretted not having extended the trip to spend the weekend with her mother in nearby Georgia. "I don't make it to the Southeast very often," she said. "It would have been so easy just to take a couple more days."

MULTIPURPOSING VERSUS ENJOYING THE "PURE" EXPERIENCE

By its very nature, bundling means compromise. For Scott Hillard, the publisher-scout master, camping with the scout troop is a different experience than either camping alone with his sons or camping with his wife or with other adult friends. He says it's worth the trade-off in order to avoid giving up the experience altogether. Tina Sosa can give a head-spinning description of the multiplicity of trade-offs involved in her nightly walk. "If I can persuade my husband to go on my walk with me, I can accomplish another goal— having a good talk with him. But he'd rather rollerblade than walk—and I'm not a big skating fan. However, we can wear the dogs out faster that way, so sometimes it's worth it. On other days when I can persuade Jeff to walk with me, it requires a different type of trade-off, because he moves much more slowly than I do—so the exercise benefit of the walk isn't as great."

Unlike their alternating counterparts, diehard bundlers are satisfied with the compromises that come with accomplishing many purposes at once. Both Sandra Gammon and Camille Harrells spent time as stay-at-home moms. "I got enough of the 'pure' experience to last a lifetime," says Sandra. Camille adds: "I think I'm a much better mother when I have other priorities in my life. To me, having a demanding job actually makes my life feel more balanced than staying at home full time. My kids and I enjoy our time together much more." Kelly Baker is not a mother but similarly avoids the boredom of single-tasking. "I don't want simplicity. I need more stimulation in my life. I'm more comfortable trying to do many things at once."

MANAGING RELATIONSHIPS WITH NONBUNDLERS

Just because the bundlers can live with the trade-offs doesn't mean their loved ones are thrilled about it. Sandra Gammon points out that her commitment to planning and coordinating can stress relationships with the nonplanners in her life. "My husband is much more of a homebody than I am," she says. "Sometimes my tendency to plan our calendar weeks in advance wears him out. He ends up wishing that we could just stay home by ourselves one evening—and only try to accomplish one thing, not seven."

Gina Caldwell, a single professional who lives in New York, recently planned a trip home with her boyfriend, Dave. They had been together for six months, and Gina was eager for Dave to see her family, the family cabin, her hometown of Minneapolis, and all the other important people in her life. She felt energized as she steered him through a maze of activities, each designed to accomplish multiple objectives. By the end of the week, she was proud of how much they had accomplished. Dave, who had planned on a relaxing week away from his hectic job, went home stressed out and exhausted.

GENERATING ENERGY VERSUS BURNING THE CANDLE AT BOTH ENDS

"I don't think that bundling works as well for introverts," says Sandra Gammon. Many of the other bundlers in our sample agreed. "Bundling won't work if you don't get energy off of coordinating a lot of activities and people," says Kelly Baker. "I think that if it takes more energy to plan and schedule than you get from doing it, it's going to exhaust you to the point that it's not worth it. It takes a lot of stamina to keep everything going in the right direction." Kelly pointed out that she's seen some people fail at bundling because they plan a calendar full of high-impact activities and then feel exhausted halfway through their agenda.

SUMMARY

As the stories and examples in this chapter suggest, there is a bundler type—a collection of skills and personality traits that extreme bundlers have in common and that border a bit on the obsessive. Being an extrovert and having a passion for both planning and efficiency are probably requirements for the most serious bundling. However, bundling can help anyone who wants to make small but consistent inroads into rebalancing his or her work and nonwork lives.

Ideas for Small-Scale Bundling

- Make a conscious effort to build efficiencies into your daily routine by planning errands, grocery shopping, going to the dry cleaners, for example, in a way that minimizes your time commitment. Combining even occasional trips will garner hours of time over the course of a year.

- If your work requires regular travel, look for ways to combine trips or build in more purposes.

- Look for ways to combine goals and objectives both at home or at work. If you'd like to start an exercise program and you'd also like more time for friends, find a friend who's interested in the same activities you are and team up. If you find yourself doing the same thing repeatedly with different groups of people at work, look for ways to reduce the frequency of the activity by broadening or combining audiences.

- Look for ways to increase the alignment between your work life and personal life. If your job requires consistent travel and all of your other priorities are tied to your local community, long-term balance might not be achievable in your current role. Think about career directions that could provide a better match.

6

Techflexing

BRADY DOMAN'S WIFE used to steel herself when he pulled into the driveway after work. He would walk in expressionless and barely acknowledge the kids. An hour later, Brady was essentially back at work, his head bent over papers from the office. "I never stopped, never took a break," said Brady of the time he was in charge of all human resources services for about 15,000 employees at a large regional bank in Cincinnati. "I was always available, 365 days a year. And the nature of the job was such that all complaints and issues came to my desk. Every day was ten hours of fighting fires."

Fortunately, when Brady's heart attack hit, the plane he was on was just passing over Albuquerque.

Brady says he would have died if he hadn't been over a major city at the time. And he would still be a walking zombie if he hadn't started then to rethink his job and his life. He and his wife already knew they wanted to move to Sedona, Arizona. So, like many balance seekers, he decided to tap the resources of modern technology and take his work off-site with him. His day starts at 6:00 A.M.—which is 9:00 A.M. at the home office. He can put in a solid two or three hours before breakfast. And his evening commute now involves little more than shutting down the computer, closing the office door, and walking down the hall to the kitchen.

Brady's home office is set up with many of the modern apparati that also adorn his colleagues' home offices in Cincinnati: a phone, a fax machine, and a computer connected to the Internet. But the difference between Brady and most of his coworkers is that he uses these technological adjuncts not just to work faster, easier, and longer but primarily to facilitate the lifestyle that he craves. "I've wondered if I should install some sort of videoconferencing capability in my home office," he muses, "but I've decided against it. I kind of like to be able to work in my pajamas."

He's part of a growing number of workers we call techflexers— those who use technology to build flexibility into their work and nonwork lives, leading to a more satisfying balance between the two.

SERVANT OR MASTER?

Cell phones, DSL lines, fax machines, e-mail, voice mail, networked computers, Palm Pilots, pagers, the Web—with a flood of new gadgets, using technology to get work done in unusual places and at odd times is a pervasive and booming trend. As with any new wave, the extremes are almost silly. Consider "telematics," the convergence of four familiar technologies—automotive, computing, wireless communications, and global positioning—to create the first true "office-in-a-car." For a tidy sum, an after-market customizer can equip your vehicle with a trunk-mounted PC, a flat-screen monitor that pulls out of your dashboard, a wireless Internet connection, cellular conference call capability, and color printer.[1] It brings a whole new meaning to the term "high-powered workstation."

Today's extremes often become tomorrow's norms, however. Taking work off-site in some form, once considered avant garde, is now mainstream. In 1999, 77 percent of large North American companies allowed employees to work at home at least some of the time.[2] By 1999, one in four U.S. households had a home office and more than 15 percent of the corporate employees said that they expected to check their voice mail and e-mail on weekends and vacations.[3]

The Internet has only made it easier to telecommute. Half of all Americans now use the Internet at home, while Europeans are leading the way in accessing the net by cell phone. By 2030, according to some estimates, the United States will include 90 million telecommuters.[4]

These statistics may sound alarming to balance seekers—as if technology were a corrosive acid, seeping into and dissolving the porous barriers with which we've attempted to compartmentalize our lives. Doesn't the lure of a twenty-four-hour, seven-day-a-week connection to our jobs, coupled with the power to work from anywhere—airplanes, hotel rooms, our cars, even that campsite in the woods—seduce us ever further from a balanced life?

It can—and for many ardent technophiles, it does. But technology can as easily be our servant as our master. A growing number of wired workers now place their work time and space where, and only where, they want it. Eighty-three percent of more than 1,000 respondents in *Fast Company*'s 1999 survey said that using the Internet and other technology was part of their strategy for work-life balance.[5]

The most obvious method of techflexing is telecommuting—but it's telecommuting with a twist. Unlike many telecommuters, techflexers don't simply do the same job, during the same hours, from home. They find ways to use the telecommuter's tools more flexibly, freeing their lives from the somewhat arbitrary constraints of an eight to five workday. They may work entirely from home, either as corporate employees or self-employed individuals. Or they may spend just one or two afternoons a week working from home.

Nor do all techflexers connect remotely to their work from a home office. Some do the opposite, using a pager, cell phone, instant messaging, or even a Webcam to stay connected to family while at work. Then there are those who use technology to simplify their personal lives. They plan vacations on the Internet, send themselves automatic birthday reminders by e-mail, order home-delivered groceries on-line, or enter Web chat rooms to meet new people.

The common theme in all of these variations is this: In the pursuit of work-life balance, techflexers make technology their ally, their enabler, even their catalyst.

To find out if techflexing might be a viable balancing strategy in your life, take the following brief Techflexing Aptitude Test.

CHARACTERISTICS OF SUCCESSFUL TECHFLEXERS

Effective techflexing doesn't require that you be a full-fledged geek. As suggested by the questions on the self-test, the strengths you need are primarily nontechnical. Let's examine these key strengths and characteristics in greater detail.

DOES YOUR COMPANY SUPPORT IT? (QUESTIONS 1 THROUGH 3)

Your ability to techflex may have more to do with your line of work than with you. Certain jobs simply can't be done from home: elementary school teacher, law enforcement officer, gene splicer, airline pilot—you could no doubt continue the list. If your job is on that list, you probably should skip the rest of this chapter or consider a job change that would allow you to work remotely.

Even if you pass this first hurdle (that is, your job could be performed from your kitchen table without anyone noticing), you've still got your employer to convince. Many organizations are hesitant to open what they fear will be a telecommuting floodgate. Meredith Long, the single mother we portrayed as an involuntary juggler in chapter 2, sees techflexing as the ideal solution to her

Techflexing Aptitude Test

Place a check mark next to each statement that you think is true for you and your current job.

✓ 1. My job can be effectively performed not only outside of the office but outside of standard nine to five business hours.

✓ 2. My company has shown support for flexible work options, including telecommuting.

✓ 3. On a typical day, I can get the same (or greater) quality and quantity of work done from home as I could from the office, especially since I have zero commute time.

✓ 4. I like to talk to people over the phone and via e-mail, and I respond promptly to voice mail.

___ 5. I know how to maintain a high-enough profile that I would not be forgotten, even if I were to spend relatively little time in the office.

___ 6. I have the discipline to enforce boundaries between my work life and my personal life, even if they were done in the same space.

___ 7. A number of my most important nonwork activities need to be done during regular working hours.

___ 8. I don't mind working alone; daily social interaction with coworkers isn't something I crave.

(Continued)

Techflexing Aptitude Test, continued

____ 9. I would call myself a self-starter; I'm motivated by projects and deadlines more than by others working around me.

____ 10. I enjoy trying out new electronic gadgets and on-line services.

Scoring: Count up the number of check marks you have made. Interpret your scores according to the following rules:

1–3 check marks: Techflexing probably will not be your most effective strategy for work-life balance.

4–6 check marks: You should at least consider techflexing as a strategy.

7–10 check marks: Techflexing is a strategy that may work extremely well for you in your quest to rebalance your life.

---

work-life tension, but it's not an option. Her company won't support it—at least not yet, for a person at her level.

Brady Doman was able to convince his company to let him telecommute from Sedona to Cincinnati, but it took some persistence:

> "When I suffered my heart attack, it really made me think about a job change. I'd gotten about as far as I could go in my present position. I saw my boss's job and was pretty sure I didn't want it. A lot of forces converged: my health, my position with the company, and we bought a vacation home in Arizona a year and half ago. We knew that's where we wanted to end up.

"So I started pitching the idea to the company. At first, my boss ignored it. I think she thought I'd forget about it. Keep in mind that our bank has no tradition of this. We are pretty late in the game in terms of getting into flexible work options. There was almost no precedent.

"About the third or fourth time I proposed creating this arrangement, I told my boss I was going to start looking for jobs in the Phoenix area if we couldn't make this happen. She finally realized I was serious."

Brady wasn't trying to hold the company hostage, but the thought of losing him got his manager's attention. He also voluntarily switched from a senior management role to that of an internal consultant in charge of program development, executive education, interfacing with university-based programs, and developing internal curricula. "I still do some coaching and organization change work," he says, "but there was no way to be a remote manager—not, at least, in our organization."

The list of reluctant employers seems to be getting shorter, however, as the evidence mounts in support of telecommuting and other off-site work. For example, in colleges and universities the traditional role of the professor was thought to require intensive face-to-face contact with students. When the idea of "e-learning" first appeared, college professors were among its loudest and most skeptical critics. But a growing number of faculty members now teach their courses exclusively over the Internet—and preliminary studies have found that students in certain on-line courses outperform their peers in the lecture hall on standard end-of-term tests.

This last point is important and needs to be translated to a non-academic setting. Techflexing will work for you and your employer *only if* it helps you achieve results greater than or equal to the results you would produce if you were in the office full time.

Otherwise, it's a social welfare program that will be eliminated the next time your company's quarterly earnings disappoint Wall Street.

CAN YOU MANAGE "REMOTE INTERDEPENDENCE"? (QUESTIONS 4 AND 5)

It sounds like an oxymoron—remote interdependence, the ability to build relationships and stay interpersonally connected with your manager, peers, and customers, all of whom you rarely, if ever, see face to face. It's a critical variable in the techflexing equation, however; without it, your impact is compromised, your reputation unknown, and your job vulnerable.

Don Hunt is a systems engineer for a Boston-based financial services giant. His manager is in Dallas, his cubicle is in Salt Lake City, yet he works all but one day a month from his home office in Park City—"a great place for skiing, mountain biking, and astronomy," he says.

Don has more phone lines (four) than children (three). An operations consultant, he fixes computer glitches across the country and sometimes in the United Kingdom. Since he communicates all day with remote clients and is constantly monitoring systems, in addition to the usual e-mail and voice mail, Don has to have constant high bandwidth Web access. Active phone and ISDN lines are Donald's extended ears and arms. Without them, he's paralyzed. With them, he enjoys the flexibility to walk his dogs, take a morning to ski on fresh powder, or simply meet a buddy to have a beer.

"Spontaneity is a big part of my definition of balance," he explains, "and technology is a huge enabler. I have a pager and a cell phone. So, when I'm on the clock, I'm never really unavailable—and in my job, availability is crucial." What really makes it work, though, is the trust he's built with his customers. "The key is to be able to provide that personal touch when you're working with people, whether it's over the phone or across the table. You have to have a relationship with them, not just a computer link."

He worked diligently at relationship building early on. "When I first started doing this [working from home], I needed to travel," he says. "It was a conscious strategy to get to know my customers, build a relationship with them, and get training in all of the pertinent technologies. I also had to show my management that this was going to work, that I was willing to do whatever it took to provide outstanding service. So that year, I flew more than 50,000 miles. Because of that investment, I now travel less. Last year, I flew just over 25,000 miles and this year, I may not even fly 15,000."

Less travel, no commute, and yet Don insists that his availability to his customers has actually increased since he started working from home. "I've had clients from Boston call me and say that they'll be working late and could I be available in the office to help them, and I say, 'No problem, I'll just go downstairs and log on.' Usually, they didn't even know that I work from home. I figure that the company gains about an hour and a half of my available time, every day."

Don's efforts to get out and meet his customers have made a huge difference in his effectiveness as a techflexer. He also reads all of his e-mail messages every day and has great phone skills. Like all successful teleworkers, he can convey the feeling that there is a human on the other end of the line.

A side benefit of being good at remote interdependence is that it helps you stay connected to the office grapevine. Politics are hard enough to unscramble when you're in the middle of them. Telecommuters, with the extra handicap of distance, need to develop a knack for having "virtual" hallway conversations with their peers.

CAN YOU MAINTAIN STRICT BOUNDARIES? (QUESTION 6)

All of the telecommuting handbooks point out that to be successful, you've got to be good at separating your job and home domains. You may like the idea of working and living under the same roof, but if you think you'll be able to strap on a headset and hold high-stakes client teleconferences while you do the laundry or weed the garden, think again.

"You're still doing business, even though you're working from home," says Carolyn Maddux, a human resources vice president for the same financial organization that employs Don Hunt. The company has moved aggressively to offer flexible work options. "At first, some of our people thought they could use remote work as a substitute for childcare. They discovered that it's almost impossible to get work done with a toddler running around."

The challenge is to keep your home life from leaking into your professional life—and vice versa. This isn't always as easy as it sounds.

Jeff Hill worked for IBM for twenty years. (He is now a full-time professor.) For ten of those years, his boss and phone extension were at headquarters in Armonk, New York; his office and computer were at his home, first in Phoenix, then in Logan, Utah. A statistician and data analysis guru, he had unique skills that earned him respect, credibility, and a lot of freedom. He would get up at 4:00 A.M. (6:00 A.M. Armonk time) and work for three hours, then take a break to go for a long run, help with breakfast, and get the children off to school. Later, he would spend another stint on the phone and at his computer during the quiet hours while the children were in school.

Most days, this schedule kept his personal and professional lives out of each other's way. On one occasion, however, the two collided.

"I was downstairs in my den, recording my office voice-mail greeting," Jeff recalls. "Working from home, you have to have a professional-sounding voice mail greeting, so everyone knows you're hard at work. Across the hall from my office is the laundry room. My wife was folding clothes at the time, and my daughter Emily, who is six, had just gotten out of the shower. She couldn't find any clean clothes in her bedroom and came down to the laundry room to find some. As my wife greeted her, the voice-mail greeting I produced sounded like this:

Male voice: "Hi, this is Jeff Hill with IBM."

Female voice: "Look at you! You have no clothes on!"

Male voice: "I'm not available right now . . . "[6]

Luckily, Jeff's mishap was easy to fix. Yet nearly all of the tech-flexers we interviewed had similar, if less comical, stories to tell. Their advice was to make sure your home office has a door that you can shut and, ideally, lock. A tangible barrier helps shield the tech-flexer from the intrusions and temptations of home. According to an on-line survey of IBM employees, those with a door on their home offices were more likely to stay on task and have less difficulty focusing while home.[7] Some even help their families understand the "rules of engagement" by posting the do's and don'ts on the office door.

The check valves are perhaps harder to keep closed when the flow is in the opposite direction. A hallmark of successful techflex-ers, however, is their ability to keep the information superhighway from flattening their lives. They've discovered how to avoid the call of the wild pager during their off-hours. It's a simple quid pro quo: they won't let barking dogs or giggling kids disrupt work-related calls; in return, they refuse to take work-related calls while they're walking the dog or playing with the kids.

Jeff Hill, who has gone on to study work-family issues in his aca-demic career, observes that all too often, workers use technology not to create a more flexible work-life mix but to increase the number of hours that they work. "They're not any better off," he says. "Home has become a mere extension of the workplace. Because of new technology, they can put in more hours, so they work faster and longer until it crowds out a private life and erodes family relationships."

Jeff was highly valued during his time at IBM, but he's more proud of the fact that he trained for and ran a marathon with one of his daughters and has spent countless hours hiking and camping with his family in Utah's Wasatch Mountains. "My profession is really important to me, but it's an offshoot of my role in the family," he says. "I'm lucky that I've found a career that lets me support my family and be with them."

WHAT ABOUT YOUR NONWORK COMMITMENTS? (QUESTION 7)

Most would-be telecommuters fail to ask themselves this question: Do my nonwork priorities really require attention during working hours? If yes, then techflexing offers clear advantages over other work-life balance strategies. It's what allows Jeff Hill to put in a full workday yet always be there for the morning rush and the afternoon sports coaching. Brady Doman has a similar schedule; unless he's on a business trip, he's there to welcome his children home from school.

Significantly, both of these men work in time zones two to three hours west of their home offices (as does Don Hunt). This creates a natural offset in their schedules, which they use to their advantage. Since their definition of balance revolves around their families, the flexible schedule is perfect. Similarly, outdoors-oriented workers often find this type of techflexing an ideal choice; it frees up some of their daylight hours for skiing, biking, sailing, and so forth.

If, on the other hand, the activities that help you feel balanced aren't daytime-specific, remote work may be a less urgent need. You may still find that techflexing is a helpful strategy but in a very different way.

Rose Jordan is a young single professional in the San Francisco Bay Area. She works full-time, occasionally overtime, fundraising and doing public relations for a nonprofit organization. Outside of work, she salsa or swing dances one or two times a week, takes tap and guitar lessons, and hunts out obscure local bands. Rose places high value on staying in touch with her family, most of whom live in Wyoming, yet her parents find it hard to catch her at home.

Instead of relying on the phone, Rose communicates with her family almost solely through Instant Messaging (IM). With IM, she can have an on-line conversation with any of her friends or family who are also on-line. Rose's mother is connected at work all day, her sister dials up frequently, and her father gets it at home. Two aunts are connected, and on her last trip home, Rose set it up for her grandparents. "Now Grandma and Grandpa camp on-line," she says.

Rose's mother doesn't like talking much over Instant Messaging while she is at work. It's too disruptive, so she and Rose only send instant messages when they need information immediately. Still, Rose can tell whether or not her mother has logged on to her computer every day. "It's just comforting to know that she's there, and that it would only take a couple of keystrokes to talk to her."

Instant Messaging gives Rose a way of staying close to her family, despite her busy evening and weekend agenda. "It's an equilibrium for me. I'll be at work all day. But as long as I can have some interaction with people I care about on-line, then it's okay."

Like Jeff Hill and Brady Doman, Rose has to be disciplined to not let her family communication become a distraction to her work;

she, too, has to maintain the boundaries. Yet she has found a very simple way to use technology to increase her daily sense of well-being.

DO YOU HAVE THE RIGHT PERSONALITY? (QUESTIONS 8 AND 9)

Personality is a loaded word for some people, but two personal characteristics correlate highly with techflexing success: your tolerance for solitude and your ability to be a self-starter.

We asked Don Hunt what advice he would offer to someone considering setting up a home office. "I'd say to look inside themselves and make sure they really don't have a high need for people interaction," he replied. "Could they really enjoy spending all day without being able to pop their head over their cube and ask their neighbor a question?"

Filtering everything through the phone and the keyboard all day can be lonely and tedious. Being able to look into the eyes of your dog while you work or having lunch with your spouse comes at the cost of spontaneous banter and joking with your coworkers. The contrast took Brady Doman by surprise:

> "I had spent 14 years with the company, made it to the level of a senior vice president—and the day I left, it was like I'd walked off the face of the earth," Brady explained. "I went from being the ultimate insider to nobody, from Mr. Connected to Mr. Unconnected—overnight, like flipping a switch. You go from having an overwhelming amount of information coming at you, to nothing. It's a real eerie feeling. The phone didn't ring, there was no mail—the silence was deafening. You have to plan for those transition issues, think about them, expect them and find a way to overcome them."

Brady's observation is quite common. In our experience, some people never can overcome the isolation of working from home.

Chris Watson, a management consultant who lives in New York City (and who is profiled in chapter 4), has decided that telecommuting isn't for her. "My company offered to set up an office in my apartment," she says. "I thought about it for about two seconds, then said 'No way!' Can you see me, trapped in that studio apartment, staring at the same four walls all day? I'd go crazy."

The second characteristic—being a self-starter—is related to the isolation. Some people have a hard time getting motivated without a manager or peers. This isn't a character flaw, just a characteristic that you're better off knowing about *before* you pack up your cubicle and go home. If the lure of the Internet, ESPN, or Oprah is just too strong without someone wandering in now and then to keep you honest, think twice about going solo.

"Success for me is accomplishing an important mission on my own," says Jeff Hill. "I get motivated by tangible work projects that are important and visible. During my time at IBM, I would do whatever it took to get outstanding results. The payoff was that my bosses gave me a lot of autonomy, because they trusted me to do high-quality work on time"—even though his office was 2,000 miles away.

ARE YOU COMFORTABLE WITH TECHNOLOGY? (QUESTION 10)

You don't have to be the neighborhood nerd to make techflexing work for you. It helps to at least be on friendly terms with technology, of course, but a spirit of adventure and some fundamental curiosity are almost more important than technological savvy. You can usually find the help you need to make things work; the question is do you know where to look?

On Sunday nights after she puts her four-year-old and five-year-old to bed, Kelly Hatfield of Quincy, Massachusetts, fixes a cup of herbal tea, sits down at her computer, and shops for groceries. It takes her about fifteen minutes on

HomeRuns.com to buy a week's worth of provisions. The next morning, a delivery person carries the large containers of food into her kitchen and unloads them wherever she wants. The produce is fresh, the bananas are the color she likes best, and the meat is cut to order.

Kelly doesn't consider HomeRuns.com a luxury. "We end up spending about the same amount as we did at the grocery store," she says. And talk about convenient: No more juggling kids in the aisles and lugging the groceries into her kitchen—which will become even more challenging now that she's pregnant with her third child.[8]

Kelly is a techflexer, not a tech-head. Her willingness to expand her comfort zone (for example, trust someone else to choose her bananas for her) saves her a lot of hassle each week. Being familiar with the use of a Web browser helps. But even if you weren't the first one on the block with an MP3 player, the sibling who always programmed the VCR, or the one who taught your friends how to do their taxes and stock trading on-line, you probably know enough to use technology as a tool. If you balance your checkbook on the computer, use your bank's Web site to download last month's statement. Buy movie tickets on-line to have more time with your spouse over dinner. If you need more ideas, ask your children.

The less you know about technology, however, the more you need to plan ahead. Brady Doman found this out the hard way. When he first set up his home office in Arizona, he ran into a few technical difficulties. "I was really naïve," he admits. "It took forever to get the e-mail and Internet connections worked out. I spent two months of nonproductive time because I couldn't get inside the company firewall. I should have started working on the IT (information technology) much sooner. My advice would be to develop a strategy for simple things like making sure you stay on e-mail lists, keeping your voice mail active, and having your regular mail forwarded well before you actually start working from home."

WEIGHING THE TRADE-OFFS

Techflexing—in its full, home-office manifestation—can offer one overwhelming benefit: the flexibility to schedule your work hours to be more in harmony with your life's other priorities. A father can take his children to school in the morning; a mother can be home when they arrive from school; a breast-cancer survivor can spend her mornings volunteering at the local hospital; a lay pastor can be available for his "flock" when they need him.

"Being able to do what you want, when you want to do it," says Don Hunt, "how can I put a price on that? I'm not wealthy. I don't have unlimited resources to 'play.' But I do have the flexibility to jump on opportunities when they present themselves. It's about being able to get up from my computer and walk my dogs between one phone call and my next meeting, to clear my head—or being able to walk upstairs, get a cup of coffee, and have it be home brew."

Don's wife has noticed in him an improved attitude and more positive outlook since he stopped driving to the office every day. This may seem like an intangible, but when quality of life goes up, it can have a cascading effect on everything else. An IBM survey of more than 9,000 employees in eleven countries showed that telecommuters, on average, reported higher levels of morale, loyalty, and—interestingly—productivity. "Employees with flexibility in the timing and location of work were able to work longer hours before experiencing difficulty in balancing their work and family life," says Jeff Hill, who participated in the study. The researchers used specific measures to illustrate the benefits. The "break point" was the number of weekly work hours beyond which employees reported feeling overwhelmed; the "balance point" was the maximum weekly work load that still allowed them to feel a sense of work-life equilibrium. Employees in flexible, telecommuting roles reported an average break point of 60 hours per week, and an average balance point of 44 hours per week. The comparable averages for those with traditional work arrangements were 52 hours per week and 41 hours per week, respectively.[9]

Such numbers translate fairly easily into direct economic benefits for the company. At-home workers also turn nonproductive commute time into productive work time. Don Hunt saves seventy miles a day and is more available to customers. According to one estimate, a company can save $8,000 per employee per year when that employee works at home.[10]

Couple these economic benefits with the lifestyle advantages and it's not difficult to see why telecommuting is a growing trend. Hewlett-Packard sees it as a way to recruit and retain talent; a full 12 percent of HP employees have formal teleworking arrangements.[11] In 1998, when the large accounting firm Ernst & Young saw that it was losing 22 percent of women professionals annually, it moved decisively to reduce the loss. One of its most successful changes was to adopt flexible scheduling and to stress results rather than face time. Eighteen percent of new partners are now flextime working mothers.[12]

As with all of the strategies for rebalancing your life, however, techflexing has its share of trade-offs. Before you start knocking out walls to make room for a home office, consider carefully the following costs.

OUT OF SIGHT, OUT OF MIND

We've already discussed the workplace isolation that comes with working from home. Techflexers can be cut off from support networks and mentors, unable to give input about policies that affect them, and left out of the informal information loop. When tough decisions are being made about promotions, special assignments, and other responsibilities, relative anonymity is not your ally. Like it or not, never showing up at the water cooler can make you a bit more vulnerable. Don Hunt says that because he misses out on hallway conversations and doesn't see people daily, "There's some loss of synergy. I try to mitigate these negatives by making a lot of phone calls."

Since they often work unseen, techflexers must have something to display at the end of the day. Sue Shellenbarger has noted in her *Wall Street Journal* column that telecommuters suffer anxiety when they feel that their productivity may be falling. The voice in their heads says, "I don't produce, therefore I am not."[13] Your coworker may barely be awake at his desk, but he'll still get credit for being on the job. Telecommuters, on the other hand, give managers few ways of evaluating them besides productivity. Their work must be substantial and measurable enough to stand alone.

For this reason, even the most die-hard techflexers we talked to say they like to keep a foot in the office door. Don Hunt still has a cubicle in the company's Salt Lake City office and goes there about once a month. Jeff Hill, after ten years of maximum autonomy, says his ideal mix would be "working four days a week at home on projects, then spending one day a week at the office to tend social and political relationships, attend meetings, and just generally keep checking in."

BYE-BYE, MANAGEMENT LADDER

Aside from missing out on promotions because managers tend to forget about them, many remote workers don't advance because they simply can't do the job from home. Working as a part of a team can be hard enough for a telecommuter; managing a team from a distance is a challenge most companies aren't willing to risk.

Of course, a supervisory job isn't the only path to a satisfying career. But if you're serious about a leadership role, you may want to moderate your telecommuting. Many successful managers find they can work from home one day a week, but not more.

Once you've tasted the freedom of a home office, however, one day a week may not be enough to satisfy you. Don Hunt still wrestles with this dilemma. "I would consider a managerial job, even though it would require a lot more in-office time," he says. "In fact, I was on the list for a management job a while back, and my boss and I were working toward it." After reviewing the situation, however, the company felt it would be unfair—to Don, his team, and the company—to give a rookie manager the job of supervising a geographically dispersed team. "And to tell you the truth," adds Don, "I'm not sure I'd want to give up the life I've created, even if it meant a nice promotion."

REDUCED COMPENSATION

Brady Doman left an executive-level job in order to telecommute. By doing so, he figures he took a 30 percent pay cut. Not that his salary was reduced; the hit came in the form of fewer stock options and a less generous bonus program. But as a heart-attack survivor, he was grateful to keep his health benefits. And the company pays for his biweekly travel to Cincinnati. "That's part of my compensation," he says, "not explicitly, but I kind of see it that way. They're paying for a key part of making this lifestyle choice work for me, and that's worth a lot."

The question to ask yourself is this: How much money would it be worth to have the kind of flexibility you seek?

SUMMARY

Techflexing is a rebalancing strategy that relies on technology in order to gain greater flexibility in one's life. The majority of techflexers are telecommuters, many of whose jobs allow them to accommodate their daily nonwork commitments without diminishing their contribution and value to their employers. For those who don't mind the solitude and whose work is amenable, techflexing offers a nearly ideal solution. They can eliminate unproductive commutes, take advantage of daylight hours for some of their personal priorities, and get their work done during the hours that make the most sense.

Like all of the strategies for work-life balance, techflexing shouldn't be taken too far. Technology isn't a replacement for face-to-face interaction, either at work or at home. But it can be a powerful tool to make more time for the interactions you're really interested in.

Ideas for Techflexing Without Telecommuting

- If you have a long commute, get a cell phone with a hands-free device. Use it to catch up with friends and family when you're on the road.

- If you have access to a laptop computer at work, manage your schedule so that you leave early and finish your on-line work at home, at your own convenience.

- Create a Web site as a way of keeping in touch with friends and family.

- Do your personal and gift shopping on-line.

- Use the Internet to make travel reservations, buy tickets for movies or other entertainment events, or to save time at the airport check-in counter.

- If you travel a lot for work and have a cell phone, distribute the number to all of your friends and family so that they can call you easily, no matter where you are.

- Get a pager so that your child or your child's school can get in touch with you at any time.

- Take advantage of on-line banking, or move to a financial management company that provides the means to track all of your accounts on a single Web site.

- Pay your bills electronically.

7

Simplifying

STERLING MARINO, now in his mid-60s, looks back on his life with few regrets. After finishing his doctorate in psychology, he had numerous job offers from top research universities and prestigious private clinics. But he chose the road less traveled and took a job as a professor and counselor at a small community college in the Monterey, California, area. His timing was impeccable—he and his wife, Jacqueline, bought land in Carmel, California, well before the Silicon Valley boom drove prices out of reach.

For thirty-five years, they have built a life centered on self-sufficiency and service. They've raised goats, chickens, rabbits, berries, and vegetables, and built their own furniture. Now retired, Sterling still works a few hours each week at the local library, teaches an adult education course in career development each quarter, and writes an occasional scholarly article. Jacqueline shares mountain biking and hiking with him, teaches enrichment courses at the local elementary school, and manages an outreach program in the community. Their children are grown, raising families of their own.

In many ways, the Marinos are archetypal examples of a life based on our final rebalancing strategy, simplifying. They've made deliberate and enduring choices about their work and nonwork lives. Their life is undeniably appealing, not so much in its particulars as in the overall sense of peace and well-being it exudes. While many of the other people featured in this book have evolved their balance strategies almost subconsciously over time, simplifiers tend to arrive at their approach after long and careful contemplation. Adopting this strategy wholesale is almost always the result of consciously choosing one's values, which may run counter to the current culture of consumerism.

To understand how someone might arrive at this point, think about the forces that have made our lives more frantic. Most of us are spending more money than ever before, a result of the rising lifestyle tide that surrounds us:

- The average home size right after World War II was 750 square feet; now it's 2,300 square feet, despite the fact that the average family size has decreased significantly. The average garage space of many homes built today is 900 square feet—bigger than the average 1940s home.[1]

- Americans spend six hours a week shopping versus forty minutes per week playing with their children.[2]

And despite unprecedented prosperity at the turn of the century, we're not necessarily experiencing heightened financial security:

- A *Los Angeles Times* poll from May 2000 showed that although 84 percent of respondents believed the U.S. economy was thriving, 40 percent of them were having difficulty paying their monthly bills.[3]

- Our national savings rate in the United States hovers around zero, while Chinese, Indian, and Pakistani workers on average save a quarter of their much smaller incomes.[4]

- The average American household carried more than $7,000 in credit card debt in 2000.[5]

To fund this spending increase, most of us work harder and longer (in general) and strive for upward mobility so that we can feed our growing appetites for material goods. Simplifiers rebalance by rejecting the notion that owning more or earning more is always better. They deliberately choose relationships and nonwork pursuits over ever-increasing ownership and purchasing power. This philosophy has grown so much over the past decade that it's now a bona fide movement. Type "voluntary simplicity" into the search field of your favorite Internet engine, and you'll find dozens of Web sites, support groups, books, newsletters, and case studies designed to help you opt out of the rat race to a more wholesome way of life.

Some simplifiers, like Sterling and Jacqueline Marino, choose this approach from the beginning of their careers. Others come to it after they've tried life in the fast lane—hence the label "downshifters," a common term in the work-life literature. One 1995 poll found that as many as 28 percent of Americans had already chosen to downshift materially in some fashion, with 86 percent of them saying they were happier as a result of having done so.[6]

Whether early or late in one's career, what simplifiers have in common is their ability to make dramatic changes to uncomplicate their personal and professional lives in order to achieve better balance. On the nonwork side, simplifiers might move to more modest homes; trade in a new, leased car for an older, used model; cut back on their social schedule; or send their children to public rather than private schools. At work, they might turn down a promotion;

shift to a part-time role; or take a position that is less absorbing, requires less travel, or allows them to operate out of a home office.

ALL THINGS IN MODERATION

Although the voluntary simplicity movement has some clear environmentalist underpinnings, not all simplifiers move to the woods and embrace Henry David Thoreau as their prophet. Some apply the principles on a more micro level. They cancel magazine subscriptions, get themselves removed from catalog mailing lists, or limit their children to one extracurricular activity each. Although simplifying almost always means sacrificing possessions and earning power for enhanced lifestyle and relationship quality, it doesn't have to be an all-or-nothing proposition. Consider the following examples:

SETTING LIMITS. Max Dahlberg accepted a job as a management consultant that meant almost weekly travel from his Denver home. Despite consistent pressure to bill more hours (and thus travel more, since his company based variable pay on billable days), Max made a conscious choice to accept a smaller bonus in exchange for spending more time at home. At the beginning of each fiscal year, he would calculate the number of days he needed to bill in order to justify his base salary and earn a modest bonus. He diplomatically said no to project work that exceeded the travel limit he had set for himself. Although this also meant saying no to an eventual partnership with the firm, he concluded that occasionally making it to one of his son's soccer games or being home for his Friday night date with his wife was well worth the cost.

ELIMINATING THE COMMUTE. When Cory Burns, an economist, accepted a new job in downtown Atlanta, his wife and three children worried about the family time he'd be giving up when they moved from their home in northern Virginia, where they lived minutes away from Cory's office. Although moving to the Atlanta suburbs would have put them more squarely in the middle of their socioeconomic peer group, they chose to live in the middle of the city, where homes are older and smaller. "It's well worth it," says Cory's wife, Marie. "If we lived farther out, Cory would spend three hours a day commuting. This way, he can even come home for lunch."

MAKING DO WITH A LITTLE LESS. Anna Pearson started her career as a recreation therapist in order to pay graduate school tuition for her husband, Randy, who is a social worker. Once Randy finished school, Anna kept working full-time, moving into more responsible and higher paying roles. At the same time, Randy's career had shifted into high gear, which made them financially comfortable but emotionally tapped out. One day, the stress of juggling childcare for their three children, meeting the needs of her mentally disabled clients, and putting up with a ninety-minute daily commute reached a boiling point.

"I realized that something had to give," she says. "When Randy and I sat down and worked through our budget, we discovered that if we reduced our childcare expenses, cut down on what we spend on clothes for me and the kids, mowed our own lawn, and ate out less, we could probably make it if I switched to part-time work." A year later, Anna gives this status report: "It's still stressful sometimes, especially when we sit down to pay the bills each month—there's not a lot left over. But I think the kids are better off because of the time I spend with them, and a lot of our expenses have actually decreased—we spend less on gas and food now, and I don't need to buy as many expensive clothes (although sometimes I still miss being able to buy anything that catches my eye)."

Although simplifying requires some obvious financial sacrifices, it also offers a number of advantages in comparison to the other strategies discussed in this book:

- Unlike outsourcing, simplifying enables riding out tough economic times. Companies that use a low-cost strategy well (such as Dell Computer or Southwest Airlines) tend to be the most recession proof because their business model is based on the assumption that times are always tough. To some extent, simplifying applies the same principle on an individual level. If your expenses and demands are always low, you don't feel the shock of belt-tightening when the overall economy slows down.

- In comparison to the other strategies, simplifying probably provides some long-term health benefits. Comedian Lily Tomlin has quipped that even if you win the rat race, you're still a rat. A broad range of research shows that stress is related to most major health problems, including heart disease and cancer. By deciding not to compete for more prestige and money, and by carefully deciding where to invest their time, simplifiers free themselves up to enjoy the benefits of reduced physical tension.

- Like bundling, simplifying can be combined with other strategies to increase balance. In fact, many of the examples we used to illustrate the other strategies in this book contain elements of simplifying. Brady Doman, the banker who techflexes, uses electronic tools to make his new life in Sedona, Arizona, work— but he also took a pay cut and accepted a less influential role. Jack and Jane Elmore, a couple introduced in the alternating chapter, moved to a less expensive community so that they could afford to take turns as the breadwinner.

- Simplifying provides a way to slow down, smell the roses, and live life more deliberately. De-cluttering your life means that you have easier access to your remaining priorities, with a more clear view of what brings you joy and satisfaction. This isn't always easy and may involve heart-wrenching choices if decisions you've made in the past are inconsistent with what makes you happy. "Maintaining a complicated life is a great way to avoid changing it," says simplicity guru Elaine St. James.[7] Simplifying may bring into focus the things that cause you pain or unhappiness. But it also opens the door to changing them.

In this chapter, we'll look at a variety of case studies based on professionals who have used simplifying as a balance strategy. We'll also discuss some of the trade-offs that come with simplifying. But first, take the following aptitude test to determine if simplifying is a logical option for you.

CHARACTERISTICS OF SUCCESSFUL SIMPLIFIERS

HAVING VALUES THAT ALIGN WITH A SIMPLE LIFE (QUESTIONS 1 THROUGH 4)

Simplifiers often choose this strategy as a result of the dissonance they feel between their own personal priorities and the values being thrust upon them by a society based on careerism and consumerism. Simplifiers tend to identify what they need money to do for them, figure out how much professional satisfaction is enough, and structure their lives accordingly.

Simplifying Aptitude Test

Place a check mark next to each statement that you believe is true of you.

____ 1. My values emphasize personal relationships and non-professional pursuits over material wealth or career advancement.

____ 2. I don't derive a large part of my identity from my job.

____ 3. I would gladly give up status or promotional opportunities at work if accepting more money or responsibility would mean having less time to spend on my other priorities.

____ 4. It's not very important to me to live in a large house with expensive furnishings and all the latest conveniences.

____ 5. I get a certain amount of satisfaction from living simply and frugally.

____ 6. I have little or no nonmortgage debt, and my monthly expenses are relatively low.

____ 7. I find it easy to budget my money and avoid impulse buying.

____ 8. My partner and/or children are comfortable living a scaled-down life.

____ 9. I am not very competitive by nature.

___ 10.   I can continue to be seen as a high performer at work, even if I put in fewer hours or turn down an occasional project or assignment.

Scoring: Count up the number of check marks you have made. Interpret your scores according to the following rules:

1–3 check marks: Simplifying probably will not be your most effective strategy for work-life balance.

4–6 check marks: You should at least consider simplifying as a strategy.

7–10 check marks: Simplifying is a strategy that may work extremely well for you in your quest to rebalance your life.

Many simplifiers willingly spend time and money on items that are important to them but forego the expense of those that aren't a priority. Take Adam Simpson, an extreme simplifier. Adam bought mountain acreage in western Montana before it became a celebrity getaway. He owns his property outright and has built a modest A-frame cabin phase by phase as he's had money and time. Adam works summers as a U.S. forest ranger, with an annual income of less than $20,000. He spends winters skiing, owns few clothes, and drives a vintage 1970s Volkswagen bus. He grows much of his own food and trades his own time for most household services that he can't provide himself. Yet he also owns state-of-the-art kayaks, canoes, mountain bikes, telemark skis, and stereo equipment. He doesn't have indoor plumbing or a washing machine, but he owns and maintains a hot tub and a sweat lodge. Some people might question the wisdom of Adam's investments, but to him they make perfect sense. "I knew at an early age what was important to me," he says, "and I spend my money accordingly."

Simplifying doesn't necessarily mean settling for a low paying job, although it probably does mean setting limits around how much time you will spend at work and how much responsibility you will agree to take on. More importantly, it means being clear about what role you want work to play in your life and being vigilant about maintaining whatever boundaries you decide to set.

"It was a real revelation to discover that my profession didn't have to fulfill all of my needs," says Madison Geery, an internal consultant for a large high-tech company in Research Triangle Park, North Carolina. "If I looked at work simply as a way to earn money, I had a lot more career options." Having been raised in a high achievement family, coming to this conclusion was no easy journey. "It was a big relief to realize that I could do a good job and succeed in work without trying to set new records for on-the-job achievement."

Madison arrived at simplifying after a lot of soul searching early in her career. "I remember the wonderful moment when I realized that I could actually choose my own values. I found that simplicity was a much higher priority for me than the ambition and achievement that I'd grown up with." Simplifying allows her the freedom and time to pursue many different interests—spending time with friends, reading, writing, or playing the guitar. While she thoroughly enjoys her job, she also loves the fact that it's not all-consuming. "I've tried to ensure that my performance at work has been consistently good. Ideally, I'll be able to keep my job long term." Good performance also buys a lot of freedom and flexibility. "I occasionally turn down optional projects that would infringe on nonwork interests," Madison points out, "even if it's just reading a good book or spending time with my partner, Barbara."

Being clear about what's most important also helps Madison choose what opportunities to turn down and how to invest her time. "Over the years, I've had calls from several volunteer organizations that would like me to be on their boards," Madison relates. "I always tell them I'm flattered to be asked—which is honestly true. Then I ask about what kind of a commitment they're looking for from me. I translate that commitment into the number of hours I'd likely have to spend, and then I calculate how much I could write in the same amount of time. When I realize the time something I might like to do would take away from the activity I want to do even more, it makes it relatively easy to say no."

Obviously, some personal values are more consistent with simplifying than others. "I feel lucky that I have simple tastes and get joy from simple pleasures," says Madison. "I like well-worn clothes and think that puttering around the house is great good fun." If doing without the latest gizmo or staying at home sounds like your worst nightmare, simplifying may bring you more stress than balance. On the other hand, if your life feels a lot more manageable when you have the freedom to do whatever you want—or do nothing at all—simplifying may add satisfaction that you can't get on the job.

MANAGING YOUR FINANCES AND OTHER MATERIAL POSSESSIONS EFFECTIVELY (QUESTIONS 5 THROUGH 7)

Like alternating, simplifying poses some obvious financial constraints. You can't minimize your work commitments and expect your income to keep escalating. At the same time, simplifiers find that financial viability is only one reason for streamlining personal expenditures.

Elaine St. James was an enormously successful real estate investor back in the 1990s. She also ran a hugely successful seminar business. But her life was out of control. She and her husband owned a sprawling country home, which was far away from their jobs—her husband commuted four hours each day. The house was becoming more of a burden than a blessing—upkeep was expensive, and the couple was rarely home long enough to enjoy their investment.

Elaine's knee-jerk answer to reducing their stress levels was to outsource. They already employed a number of household helpers. Why not pay someone to prepare their meals? Although the couple could easily afford another staff member, Elaine's husband questioned her approach. "You already spend so much time managing the housecleaner, the gardener, and the bookkeeper. Now you want to manage a cook?"

The couple concluded that they didn't need more help—they needed fewer problems. So they moved to a smaller home, got rid of seldom used possessions, and began a move to overall simplification, including cutting an hour off of each ten-hour work day. As they became more devoted to their new lifestyle, advocating simplicity eventually turned into a new career for Elaine.[8]

With increased prosperity has come an increased accumulation of goods. Many U.S. families can no longer contain their possessions in their homes. The self-storage industry has expanded fortyfold since the 1960s, with more than 30,000 storage sites now in use.[9] Simplifiers have shunned unnecessary accumulation of stuff, partly because it reflects an investment of money that has little impact on quality of life or satisfaction. Looking for material efficiencies is more than just living frugally, however. Having fewer possessions means less maintenance and less hassle—hence the Zen-inspired phrase, "We think we own things, but they actually own us." Smaller homes not only cost less to buy, but they also take less to clean, maintain, and heat or air condition. Avoiding the urge to buy the latest entertainment equipment means less guilt for not having time to use it.

Simon Storz, 45, is a music teacher at one of the largest private K–12 schools in the Salt Lake City metropolitan area. He and his wife, Clee, a former high school math teacher, married late. Both wanted children, and with a little luck and planning, they had four children in six years—two single births and a set of twins.

At first glance, their lifestyle looks traditional: a money-earning husband, with a wife who engages in full-time childcare and homemaking. Both are active in community activities. Clee coaches soccer, while Simon runs a concert series for the community and writes children's plays and musicals. Clee, who served a Mormon mission in Argentina, maintains a high level of Spanish fluency and volunteers to help integrate Spanish-speaking immigrants into the community. She also bottles fruit, sews, bakes bread, stockpiles made-from-scratch freezer meals, cuts her children's hair, and is a frugal manager. Through intensive shopping, she recently found a salvaged late-model Toyota van for one-third its original price.

In describing their lifestyle, the Storz's didn't once use the word "simple." Rather, they talked about how they have consciously planned their lives and decided to do without the trappings of success. They live in a modest house, drive older (or salvaged) cars, and keep their outdated furniture, so that Simon's income provides an adequate living with a little left over. When Simon is home, he's fully engaged as a parent and partner—helping the children with their music, playing with them, cooking, and housecleaning. They take on long-term educational and recreational projects with their children— reading the *Chronicles of Narnia* series, backpacking and hiking every Saturday in the summer and skiing every Saturday in the winter.

Simon enjoys his career, and both Simon and Clee take it seriously; but they have arranged their affairs to allow time for a robust nonwork life. They have downscaled their expenses and constructed roles around intensive parenting and rich personal lives. They invest heavily in their children's education by spending time more than money—they regularly attend concerts and plays but look for free dress rehearsals or events that are underwritten or sponsored by the community. While not everyone would welcome the challenge of shopping for budget vehicles or canning fruit, Clee finds investing in her home and family a more appealing alternative than a career outside the home.

Madison Geery, the high-tech consultant, recalls a major step in her own move to more material austerity. "I was working at a seminary, where several of my friends were studying to become ministers. When one couple got ready to move, I noticed that they gave away many of their possessions." Madison recalls that this made her realize how much she could live without. She went home, packed up several thousand dollars worth of her own books, and gave them away to the local library and to the graduate program where she had studied. "It was hard letting go—I loved those books. But the truth is, nearly thirty years later, I like simplicity more than I like clutter."

Madison's commitment to de-cluttering has grown over time: "One day I was sitting on our patio, reading a book on simplifying and organization. By the time I had finished the book, I had moved seven pieces of furniture out of the house." The furniture she discarded was perfectly useful, but it was taking up space and taking up maintenance and cleaning time. The house looked simpler without it. Now she takes an annual inventory of all of her possessions and tries hard to give away anything that she doesn't treasure or use.

MANAGING RELATIONSHIPS EFFECTIVELY (QUESTIONS 8 THROUGH 10)

As with most of the strategies we've presented, simplifying comes with its share of relationship challenges—both at home and at work. Adam Simpson, the forest ranger from Montana, found this out the hard way when his marriage broke up, in large part over his commitment to simplicity. "When we first got together, we both wanted the same things," he recalls. "But over time, my wife's values changed. She started being more concerned about what we owned and how much money we made."

Simon and Clee Storz's marriage works precisely because they share a strong commitment to having a simple but multifaceted life. "This wouldn't work if we weren't a team," says Simon. "Clee's contribution to our lifestyle is every bit as important as my own. And her willingness to live modestly makes it possible for me to live my dream of being a teacher." The same could be said for the Marinos, introduced at the beginning of the chapter. They have bonded because of their lifestyle, not in spite of it.

One major challenge for families arises as children develop expensive tastes that can't necessarily be accommodated by a simplifier's budget. As children and adolescents are continuously bombarded by the media and surrounded at school by friends with different values, it may be difficult to convince them that they don't need to wear the latest styles or own the newest gadgets. Adopting a simplifying strategy may also mean making less than the maximum investment in children's future. Trade-offs here may include requiring offspring to choose in-state tuition over private universities (unless they can earn scholarships to cover most of the costs) or minimizing the number of lessons or activities they participate in during childhood.

Many simplifiers have found that one of the biggest relationship challenges comes in saying no to opportunities that sound interesting but that don't fit in with their values and priorities. This can be especially true at work because turning down assignments or scaling back commitments doesn't sit well with most managers. Adam Simpson has found that mastering many skills makes him marketable, which gives him the freedom to walk away from a job if it doesn't fit his needs. "I can think of seven jobs that I could get today," he says and then lists off some of the options. "None of them would make me rich, but I could maintain my current lifestyle with any of them."

Madison Geery takes a different approach. She's worked for the same company for almost twenty years, and has always been seen as a high performer. "I try to focus my attention on projects and assignments that will have the most impact," she says. "I try hard to keep work to only forty hours per week—which in my profession and industry is almost unheard of. But if I manage my time well and prioritize, I can accomplish as much in that forty hours as I might otherwise do in fifty or sixty hours." Madison also has found that good work and responsiveness earn flexibility and freedom. "I sometimes volunteer for particularly odious tasks. When a coworker resigned from her very specialized position, no one in our group had any desire to take on her responsibilities. I told my manager that I'd be happy to cover that area until we hired someone full time. While I didn't love doing it, I learned some new and interesting skills. More importantly, I took a load off my manager's shoulders, which is always appreciated."

One way of simplifying relationships is to minimize the variety of contacts you try to manage, while maximizing the quality of the ties that you choose to maintain. In his book *Bowling Alone,* Robert Putnam notes that many people have cut back on their commitments to clubs, service organizations, churches, political parties, and other organizations so that they can have more personal and family time.[10] Depending on your profession, the same approach may work on the job. While extensive networks may make employees in many roles more valuable, simplifiers can invest in high-impact relationships at work while minimizing their social time with other colleagues, customers, or vendors.

WEIGHING THE TRADE-OFFS

As with the other strategies, simplifying has trade-offs. The philosophical opposite of juggling (trying to have it all), simplifying by definition means giving up quite a lot. This chapter has looked in detail at some of the obvious sacrifices—less pay, less affluence, and lower professional aspirations. Look through the following trade-offs to see if simplifying is something you can live with.

DOING A LOT OF A FEW THINGS VERSUS A LITTLE OF EVERYTHING

This trade-off no doubt seems obvious, but it's worth restating. When you choose simplifying, you choose depth over breadth. It's hard to say no when what you're giving up—whether it's an interesting or challenging project, a meaningful volunteer assignment, or a big raise with more influence—is genuinely appealing. Implementing a simplifying strategy is a lot like sticking to a rigorous diet—a rich dessert may be awfully tempting, even when you know that it's not a part of your master plan. It still takes willpower and discipline to talk yourself out of attractive options.

The payoff for making this choice often comes from deepening key relationships. Many Europeans note that Americans seem to have many acquaintances and few friends. Simplifiers may opt for having fewer friends and social relationships, while reaping greater benefits because of the family-like support of the ties they choose to maintain.

EGO GRATIFICATION VERSUS A LOWER MAINTENANCE LIFE

One motto associated with the voluntary simplicity movement is "Want Less, Do Less, Be Less." Most of us can understand the first two mandates at a conceptual level, even if we don't embrace them. But to deliberately be less? Isn't that somehow refusing to live up to our potential?

"I reached a point where I felt like I was getting in my own way," says Madison Geery. "One day it occurred to me that in the overall scheme of things, I'm not that important and I don't want to inflate my value in this world. When I gave up the need to be Master of the Universe, it was surprising how easy it became to stop doing things and acquiring things that weren't that important to me."

DISCIPLINE VERSUS SPONTANEITY

"Simplifying is really a process of planning how to invest your time and money in order to bring about consequences that will uncomplicate your life," summarizes Madison Geery. Like most of the simplifiers we met, Madison plans her time carefully—both at work and beyond work. "I have a goal setting structure where work is a small part of the overall plan. On a weekly basis I plan out how I'm going to be a better partner and friend, how I'm going to pay attention to my gifts in music and writing, and how I'm going to serve other people in the community. If I don't plan for my other priorities, work has a way of taking over." A lot of simplifying is anticipating problem situations and heading them off in ways that consume less time and energy. It's a lot simpler to clean out the rain gutters when the sun is shining, although many people aren't motivated to do so until it's pouring rain and the gutters are backed up.

Because a simplified life is usually experience rich but resource poor, it takes careful planning and resource management. If you don't have the requisite skill and desire, simplifying may make your life miserable and cost you time and energy that robs you of the balance you're looking for.

SUMMARY

Simplifying isn't for everyone. Despite its growing popularity, it requires trade-offs and sacrifices that seem unreasonable to some people. However, simplifying can be used in moderation to augment any rebalancing strategy. Keys to making it work include

- Being clear about your values and priorities and managing your resources in alignment with those priorities

- Minimizing time and money wasters such as too much clutter, which requires maintenance, use, and repair that is often disproportionate with its payoff in terms of enjoyment or meaning

- Exercising discipline in saying no to people, opportunities, and things that don't fit into your master plan

- Maintaining a level of order that enables a more efficient use of time and money

- Paying dues or making investments with those who play a critical role in your life, who are not simplifiers

In this chapter, we've talked mostly about committed simplifiers, with superficial references to their more casual counterparts. But simplifying makes a good add-on strategy in an overall rebalancing plan. A list of ideas for using simplifying on a scaled-down basis is found on the next page:

Ideas for Incremental Simplifying

- Move closer to your work or work from home.

- Minimize business travel (a strategy that has gained much greater acceptance since the events of September 11, 2001).

- Get more out of your possessions—repair items instead of replacing them, buy a few high quality clothes and wear them longer before buying new ones.

- Say no to volunteer or social opportunities that don't provide the highest value for you.

- Look for roles at work where you can work more independently and where other people don't rely on you for day-to-day direction or support.

- Focus on the highest impact areas at work; strive to make more of a difference in less time.

- Decide which relationships are the most important in your life. Invest in them, and spend less time with friends or associates who bring less value to your life.

- Adopt more simple, less-expensive hobbies (for example, walking versus golf).

- Landscape your yard so that it requires less maintenance.

- Simplify your entertainment and holiday celebrations.

PART THREE
Rebalancing Your Life

8

Question Your Assumptions

"WHY ARE YOU AMERICANS so obsessed with work?" asks Francoise Pascaud, sitting across from her U.S. colleague at a small bistro in Lyon, France. "It's crazy. You're already the most powerful nation on earth. What more are you trying to prove?"

Francoise's question is mostly good-natured ribbing, but there's a serious side to it. Her life is one of enviable professional accomplishment. She is a respected professor at a reputable business school, a single mother of two young children, a researcher, a consultant, and an active patron of the arts, especially theatre. She typically spends from 8:30 A.M. to 7:00 P.M. on the job, five days a week. Yet ask her how many nights or weekends she spends doing work, and the immediate answer is, "None." The number of job-related phone calls or e-mail messages she answers at home? Zero. How often does she take less than her government-mandated five weeks of annual vacation? Never—in fact, she usually takes six weeks off, plus all of her national holidays.

"You French are spoiled rotten," is her U.S. friend's rejoinder—but he's thinking, "How can she get by with such minimal effort? If I did that, I'd be seen as a slacker."

We've spent the bulk of this book examining the forces behind—
and alternatives to—juggling. Our data and examples have been
overwhelmingly North American. What about the rest of the world?
Are U.S. workers—the hardest working on earth, according to the
United Nations study cited in chapter 1—the only ones who feel
their lives are out of control?

Certainly not. We've done research in France, Italy, Romania,
Russia, Poland, Kenya, Japan, China, Thailand, and Venezuela. In
each country, we find busy professionals with intense careers and
demanding personal lives. Rebalancing is an issue in all of these cultures, although the ways people approach it are refreshingly different from the widespread juggling we see in the United States. We
are convinced that these differences hold important lessons for balance seekers everywhere.

Interestingly, the differences have to do with the context within
which people rebalance their lives—their society's expectations
about work and nonwork pursuits and individual beliefs about the
nature of success. Religious traditions play a part in this process, as
do family patterns, economic conditions, and government inter-
ventions. Some of these ideas from other countries are more applicable to life in the United States than others. A stressed-out worker in
Boston, for example, can't instantly start behaving as if she lived
in Bangkok.

Or can she? As you read through these international examples,
we recommend that you put your own assumptions on trial. Is the
way you're thinking about the balance issue helping or hindering
your efforts to rebalance your life? You may discover in other cultures a philosophy or approach that simply makes more sense.

FRANCE: THE SANCTITY OF TIME OFF

At first glance, Jean-Luc and Pascale Dupuis look an awful
lot like jugglers. They live in France's second largest city, Lyon,

where Jean-Luc is a professor of psychology at l'Université de Lyon
and also has a private practice in the late afternoons and evenings.
He sees patients weekly in Geneva, an hour and a half away via
France's superfast train, the TGV. Pascale, a professor of organizational behavior, also does a fair amount of consulting. She travels to
Paris perhaps once a week (a two-hour trip on the TGV). Work-
related dinners, usually once or twice a week, will keep her out till
11:00 P.M. They have two children, 18-year-old Marcel and 15-year-
old Brigitte.

The Dupuis' version of juggling differs from the U.S. version in
one key aspect, however—the sanctity of time off. "We work like
crazy people during the week," says Pascale, "but the weekends are
just for us and we catch up. Jean-Luc is more of a workaholic than
I, but on weekends, even he would not dare go to his study or miss
the dinner hour. Sometimes he tries to get out of Saturday family
activities, but the children are quick to confront him."

As a result, Saturday is a relaxed day of running errands, doing
grocery shopping, and catching up on household chores, in which
the parents and children are equally involved. Saturday evening is
reserved for dinner with a small group of close family friends. "No
one even thinks of doing work-related entertaining on weekends,"
says Pascale. Sunday is likewise a family day. The four of them often
play tennis together or go swimming. Most of their extended family is nearby, and typically they have lunch with relatives and a
leisurely afternoon of talking.

Jean-Luc and Pascale also have a sharp demarcation where vacations are concerned. As a family they spend three weeks together
on the Côte d'Azur every summer and a week in the French Alps
skiing every winter. National holidays, such as Bastille Day and the
All Saints Day four-day weekend, are also strictly reserved for relaxing with family and friends.

This model is typical of most French professionals. Although
they work hard, their professional lives have definite boundaries

and do not intrude into their private lives. Techflexing is unattractive to them, despite the availability of affordable Internet connections and the ubiquity of mobile phones. The French see these as work tools that would pollute their home environment. Corporate policies, which often are government mandated, reinforce the separation of work and family. If you tried to get into your office on a weekend or over a holiday, you would likely find the entrance gates closed and the building locked up, preventing you from accessing your workstation even if you wanted to. Monday through Friday, government inspectors are known to make spot checks and issue steep fines if companies are working people more than the prescribed thirty-five hours per week.

Perhaps this seems a bit extreme. But consider the results: French workers are the most efficient in the world, according to the same U.N. research that shows U.S. workers put in the longest hours.[1] French workers average $33.71 of value added per hour; U.S. workers (in third place, after the Belgians) average $32.84. The implication is that you might be more productive if you *avoid* working during evening, weekend, holiday, and vacation time.

JAPAN: "WHOLE-LIFE" BALANCE

The Japanese language has no word for "balance" in the sense U.S. careerists would use it. To communicate equal attention to personal, relationship, and work issues, they just borrow the English term and give it a Japanese ending: *baransu.* Finding individual balance is an imported, American idea. As with many aspects of Japanese culture, balance is more of a collective concept. The family unit is balanced because the husband focuses on work and the wife focuses on home and family responsibilities. With this view, the family can remain in balance even in situations of *tanshinfunin,* when the husband's job transfers him to another city or even overseas, while the wife and children remain in the family home.

Asian cultures with a base in Confucian ethics (including Japanese) also maintain that balance applies to an entire life, not to life as it is lived each day. For example, it is honorable to work very hard while able; but in old age, people should cease strenuous efforts, nap in the garden when they like, and receive honor. Society is in their debt at this time. Even though specific seasons seem out of balance, life as a whole shows balance.

For Japanese women, the concept of whole-life balance often manifests itself as seasonal concentrations. A well-educated woman will often work until she has reached a certain comfortable level in the company before she marries. She can then remain employed at that level, even if she has children. More commonly, she will forsake her career after eight to ten years, having achieved a high clerical ranking. Choosing different activities at different life-stages is her attempt to find the greatest balance.

Colleagues who drink and socialize together—a long-standing tradition in Japan—also are seeking a form of balance. One's profession and employer are critical components of personal identity. When Japanese workers combine after-hours "shop talk" with interpersonal bonding and relationship building, they are in effect bundling.

RUSSIA/UKRAINE: THE BABUSHKA EFFECT

In Kiev, at the International Management Institute, a group of Russian and Ukrainian managers are discussing personal-professional balance with their American professor. They're a hard-working group, investing long hours in their careers in order to rise above their countries' economic doldrums. Most are married, with children; nearly all of their spouses work outside the home. Yet none seem preoccupied with balance. The professor finally asks, "What gives?"

"Ah, you don't have babushkas in the United States, do you?" they respond. "We all have our parents living with us. They're part of the family, and their role is to raise our children. Most of us were raised by our babushkas, while our parents worked. When we retire, we'll raise our grandchildren. That's just how it's done. Small children are raised by their grandparents. It gives us great freedom to work during our most productive years."

Clearly, this represents a significant cultural difference; in the United States, it's not unusual to see bumper stickers proclaiming "Mother-in-law in trunk." But rather than live under the same roof as their in-laws, many busy American couples have rebalanced their lives by moving closer to their parents or extended family—a form of nonmonetary outsourcing.

THAILAND: THE MIDDLE PATH

Balance is deeply ingrained in Thai culture. Ninety percent of Thais are Buddhist. Their religion teaches the wisdom of the "middle way," first articulated by Siddartha Guatama in the fifth century B.C. While meditating under a tree, the Buddha was enlightened and understood that neither self-denial nor sensory pleasures would lead to happiness. Hence, the middle way is the way of oneness and peace, a path marked by ethical conduct, mental discipline, and the pursuit of wisdom rather than material goods.

In a recent study of 720 Thai employees and managers, 25 percent of those surveyed declared balance as their dominant career orientation. Security was more prevalent at 55 percent.[2] This could be a reflection of the ongoing Asian financial crisis, which has cooled the once-overheated Thai economy and made steady, consistent employment more of a career goal. Equally likely, however, is the "fish in water" phenomenon: Fewer Thai professionals crave balance because more of them already eat, drink, and breathe it.

Business students at Chualalongkorn University (one of the best in Thailand) explain it this way: "Balance is our life goal, not just a career goal. Sometimes we must take our minds or bodies 'off-line' to renew our spirits. Indeed, our spiritual life takes time and energy and is as important as work. So are our families and friendships. Beyond these, we work hard and seek to achieve much."

VENEZUELA: FAMILY COMES FIRST

Family values run deep in many cultures—including the United States. But whereas we often let business norms outweigh family considerations, other cultures are less willing to do so.

Venezuelans, for example, understand that few business needs are more important than family issues, and they act accordingly. When IESE, a top business school in Caracas, administered Brookyn Derr's "Career Success Map" self-assessment to a group of 500 managers (men and women), the results were staggering. Balance was the dominant career orientation for 84 percent of them—more than double what we see in the balance-oriented United States.[3] (The other orientations are security, freedom, challenge, and advancement.)

These lopsided findings surprised us, but they were entirely predictable to Elena Granell, Director of the Human Resources Institute at IESE. "When faced with a choice between staying at work and attending to a family matter, family always comes first," she says. "Everyone knows that. It's accepted, even expected."

In the United States, interrupting the typical workday in order to attend to children or aging parents raises fewer eyebrows now than it once did. Women, especially at progressive companies, are now given some leeway in this regard; for men, it remains a delicate issue. It's worth assessing how big a risk you would be taking if you push for greater flexibility. Can you think of people in your company who have found ways to fit their work around family commitments, rather than vice versa, and remain high performers? If so, sticking your neck out a little may not be the career-limiting move you thought it was. Techflexing is the strategy that allows greatest flexibility in attending to nonwork concerns.

SWEDEN: PRESERVING VALUE THROUGH RENEWAL

An executive for one of Sweden's largest corporations finds the U.S. mentality toward work puzzling. "American managers always talk about how their people are their most important asset, but they don't act that way," he says. "They do a lot of things that burn people out. You'd never do that with your manufacturing equipment. Maintenance and renewal are essential—for people as well as machines."

This executive supervises manufacturing facilities all over the world. "Our U.S. plants are productive, but it tends to be productivity through longer hours," he says. "I don't feel they're any more effective than our workers in Sweden, who put in far fewer hours." Swedes tend to view people as renewable resources. Vacation time, for example, isn't so much a reward for hard work but an important investment in people's productive capacity.

Other European nations have similar approaches. The average employee in the United Kingdom takes twenty days of vacation per year, as do Dutch workers. The average is twenty-five days per year in France and Sweden, and thirty days in Austria, Denmark, and Finland.[4] Contrast this to the United States, where employees take an average of ten vacation days per year—even though they may be entitled to many more. Committing to use all of your vacation and holiday time over the course of a year can make a difference in your overall sense of work-life balance.

CHINA: DEFERRED GRATIFICATION

"Not now!" These two words sum up the reaction of most Chinese professionals when we've presented our ideas about work-life balance. "Don't waste my time—I'm too busy ensuring my future success to worry about balance at the moment."

In Chinese culture, a dominant value is to provide the best education possible for one's children—no matter the sacrifice required. Once this goal has been achieved, balance may be considered. This is a seasonal model, in which work-life balance is achieved over the course of a lifetime. A relaxing nonwork life is reserved for people in their twilight years and becomes a time when they can travel, read, exercise in the morning, and receive honor and attention from their well-educated and successful children.

POLAND: ONE STEP AT A TIME

Magda, a plucky, energetic entrepreneur in Krakow, was working with one of the authors (Brooklyn) to review her career options. Brooklyn saw great potential in the young woman and explored a variety of ideas with her: international consulting, investing in computer technology, graduate-level education, and the licensing or franchising of her business. But, he explained, each choice would require difficult trade-offs between maximizing Magda's income and optimizing her flexibility and work-life balance.

Magda thought for a while, then responded, "You know, my husband and I have worked very hard just to get our own apartment. Next, we would like to buy a refrigerator. Then a washing machine, and eventually, a car. We'll get back to your ideas about flexibility and balance after we have the basics covered. Right now, those just aren't our biggest concerns."

We see two vital lessons in Magda's realistic, one-step-at-a-time approach. First, don't try to rebalance your life overnight. Pick one idea to implement and follow through until it becomes habitual. Relish the small payoff in your overall sense of well-being. Then pick another idea and implement it. In the words of Madison Geery (a simplifier introduced in chapter 7), "Start small and back off from there." Over time, small changes if *consistently followed* add up to big improvements.

Even more important, Magda's story offers a much-needed reality check. To those scrabbling for survival, angst about work-life balance can seem petty, decadent, even bourgeois. Rebalancing one's life is a preposterous notion for the vast majority of the world's workers—a luxury they cannot even imagine. That you have time to read this book suggests you have much for which to be grateful: food on the table, decent shelter, reliable transportation, running water, and some leisure time. Keep this in mind as you move on to the final two chapters—a diagnosis of your current state of imbalance (chapter 9) and a methodology for rebalancing (chapter 10).

SUMMARY

What can North Americans learn from other cultures?

- From the French and the Swedes, we learn that it is possible to work hard and effectively when we are at work and take advantage of evenings, weekends, vacations, and holidays to renew and rebalance our lives. Such time-outs usually follow natural rhythms and come when our bodies, minds, and spirits need a break. In effect, this is a form of alternating.

- The Japanese and Chinese teach us that rebalancing can be seasonal. It is possible to work hard while we are young and able, reserving rest and recreation for the twilight years. This can also be seen as a form of alternating.

- The Thai method of rebalancing is more holistic and philosophical. They move in and out of work, relationships, and self-development (of mind, body, and spirit) as a more continuous process. Compared to juggling, continuous rebalancing is less efficient but perhaps more effective, bringing long-term benefits to the whole person.

- A way to outsource that doesn't require millionaire status is to increase family interdependence or to be more communal, as in the Russian babushka model.

- Putting family and relationships first, as in Venezuela, may seem disruptive to professional accomplishment. By techflexing, however, it is possible to have greater freedom to take care of intensive nonwork needs.

- Finally, the Polish example reminds us of the limits to rebalancing our lives. Few professions or occupations are exempt from the dues-paying process. Going off the deep end to maximize our nonwork selves can be precarious. We may end up in uninteresting or unfulfilling careers—or worse, in the unemployment line. Being a high-performer at work is a tremendous enabler in the rebalancing process. Be wise and realistic; seek out small wins.

Edgar Schein points out that if we can understand our basic assumptions—which are mostly taken for granted and embedded in our national cultures—we can begin to make deeper, more meaningful choices about our future.[5] Questioning what we thought was the only way often opens the door to fresh alternatives. Hopefully, as we become more global, we can learn from the cultural perspectives of others.

9

Assess Your Imbalance

"WHERE DO I START? Often (actually all the time) I feel like I'm a tiny creature hanging on to those spikes at the tip of the tail of a stegosaurus," explained one Yakima, Washington, working mother. "The stegosaurus is fighting an enemy and is flailing its tail like mad. I'm gripping the spikes with all my might, trying not to get thrown off. Occasionally the dinosaur hits its attacker. Then I really get jarred. Then it's back to furious flailing. That is how I feel trying to keep up with everything. It's crazy! And I used to worry that I would grow up and be bored."

Riding the tail of a stegosaurus may not be exactly what your life feels like right now, but chances are you can relate to this woman's first question: "Where do I start?" If you've decided that you want to rebalance your life, what do you do next?

A recent PBS documentary entitled *Juggling Work and Family* with Hedrick Smith explored the problems caused by our increasingly frenetic lives. The program focused on corporate initiatives that attempt to make life more livable for employees by offering on-site childcare, flexible work arrangements, and generous sabbatical policies. Some governments also go a long way to mandate increased balance by requiring employers to provide long-term parental leave and lengthy vacations or by providing a more substantial safety net for economic hard times. But for most governments outside of western Europe and for most companies (especially the small- to medium-sized firms that employ the vast majority of workers), effective policy or program solutions that lighten or share the balance burden seem to be a long way off. Even when corporate or government solutions are available, most of them work best when they're incorporated into an individual strategy for overall life management.

Solving the balance dilemma is a never-ending process. The variables are in constant flux. Our internal career values and external career realities inevitably change and evolve over time, with the external circumstances changing more often and usually more dramatically. The dynamics of the new economy and evolving social forces combine to make juggling an ever-seductive (albeit often ineffective or unsustainable) default approach. The strategies identified in this book (alternating, outsourcing, bundling, techflexing, and simplifying) can be a systematic way to discipline ourselves against the lure of trying to do and have it all, all of the time, which leaves us with overstuffed lives.

In this chapter, we'll consider the practical application of the strategies by looking at the following questions:

- Which strategies are you using now?

- What strategies best fit your personal style and preferences?

- What works best right now, given your career and life stage?

- What strategies will you need later on, as your circumstances change?

By answering these questions, you'll be able to start making decisions about how to rebalance.

WHICH STRATEGIES ARE YOU USING NOW?

As you read this book, you may have smiled with recognition at our description of one particular strategy. However, chances are you use multiple strategies in concert. Based on the hundreds of people we studied in our research for this book, we developed the following assessment to measure which strategies you depend on the most.[1] To see your own personal profile, complete and score the self-assessment below. Or, if you prefer, point your Web browser to the following URL to take the survey and have your scores automatically tabulated on-line: www.beyondjuggling.com.

THE BALANCE STRATEGIES PROFILE (BSP)

Each item contains two statements. You must choose one of the statements, even though you may not like either or you may like both. Many of the statements will sound repetitive. The purpose of the instrument is to compare one strategy to five other strategies, so you can expect to see items that look similar in different comparisons. Do not skip any pair of statements or circle both alternatives in one set. Circle the letter corresponding to the one sentence you think best describes a tactic or strategy you currently use. Do not spend a lot of time weighing your answers.

1. I work very hard at my career right now so that I can have time for my personal life later (or vice versa).

    Computer technology allows me to work from home as much as or more than I go to an office, and this helps me achieve work-life balance.   E

(Continued)

2. I make conscious choices to gain balance by reducing the complexity in my life.   F

    I try to "have it all" in life by working harder, playing harder, and sleeping a little less.   A

3. I spend quite a bit of money on personal and household services so that I can focus my nonwork time on the most meaningful aspects of my life.   C

    I try to manage my time and my schedule with maximum efficiency, to meet all the demands of my work and nonwork lives, without missing out on anything.   A

4. In order to reduce stress, I have reduced the demands in my life.   F

    Technology is a tool I rely upon to provide the flexibility that allows me to balance my work and leisure time.   E

5. I deliberately find nonwork activities that accomplish more than one purpose. (For example, I exercise with friends, which improves my fitness and builds my relationships.)   D

    Over time, I achieve balance in "chunks." During one chunk of time (weeks, months, years), I focus on my work. Then I devote a chunk primarily to my personal life, and so on.   B

6. Rather than "have it all," I have stepped away from the fast-paced demands of life and enjoy a more slow-paced lifestyle.   F

    I make full use of my financial resources or social/family networks to delegate tasks that don't require my participation.   C

7.   I try to be fully involved in both my work and nonwork lives. I don't want to sacrifice engagement in either arena.   A

I rely on the latest technology (Internet, e-mail, cell phone, fax, etc.) so that I don't have to be at the office during regular working hours. This gives me the flexibility to maintain balance.   E

8.   Kill Two Birds with One Stone could be my motto when it comes to work-life balance. (One example might be a recreational activity that also provides community service.)   D

There are a lot of nonwork matters in which I don't feel a need to be personally involved, so I hire them out— and this helps me achieve work-life balance.   C

9.   I make changes in my life to decrease complexity and overload.   F

I switch back and forth between focusing on professional and recreational activities over periods of weeks, months, or years.   B

10.   Technology is critical to helping me achieve more balance in life.   E

Being involved in activities that fill multiple needs at once helps me to achieve more balance in life.   D

11.   I'm putting my emphasis on nonwork activities at this stage in life and later I can focus on my career (or vice versa).   B

I hire out or delegate many tasks in order to achieve better balance.   C

(Continued)

I PREFER TO:

12. Accomplish all tasks (work and nonwork) myself without eliminating anything in my life. A

    Take a minimalist approach in my lifestyle. (For example, I avoid accumulating excessive material possessions and making unnecessary commitments.) F

13. Deliberately use the peaks and valleys in my work schedule to fill my professional downtime with rich nonwork experiences. B

    Manage my personal life by purchasing services or delegating some chores to others. C

14. Handle all my work and nonwork demands myself. A

    Plan my nonwork activities carefully so that they help me "charge my batteries" in multiple ways at once (e.g., do volunteer work with a group of friends). D

15. Delegate (to a partner, extended family member, or hired help) activities that don't require my personal involvement. C

    Invest in technology that will free me up from having to work a traditional "nine to five" work schedule. E

16. Put my personal life on the back burner for a while and throw myself into my work (or vice versa). B

    Try and have it all by doing the best I can in both my work and personal life. A

I PREFER TO:

17.	Use technology to enhance my flexibility, which increases my work and personal satisfaction.	E
	Decline invitations for various activities in order to reduce complexity and be more satisfied with my life.	F

18.	Find other people to help me deal with the demands of life.	C
	Do fewer things, but get more out of them.	D

19.	Have it all by simultaneously managing all the demands of life.	A
	Use technology to help me balance.	E

20.	Put my emphasis on nonwork (or career) issues at this stage in life and later I can focus on my career (or nonwork) life.	B
	Engage in activities that help satisfy multiple demands at one time.	D

21.	Decrease the demands of life in order to invest more time in key relationships.	F
	Maintain important relationships by involving significant others in activities such as work, community service, fitness, or entertainment.	D

(Continued)

IT IS IMPORTANT FOR ME TO:

22. Arrange my life in cycles: intensive focus on work, followed by intensive focus on personal life, followed by intensive work, and so on.   **B**

Keep current with the latest technology, in order to find even better ways to maximize my flexibility.   **E**

23. Identify activities that can be performed by others. This allows me to have more time for activities that require my attention and attendance.   **C**

Make sacrifices (such as reduced income or compromised advancement in my career) to accommodate my nonwork priorities.   **F**

24. Have it all, which is why I try to keep up with all the demands of my work life and my personal life.   **A**

Make fewer commitments in my personal life but "leverage" the things to which I do commit (i.e., do more than one thing at the same time).   **D**

25. Be able to put my work on the back burner to pursue other interests (and vice versa).   **B**

Eliminate less important activities to help me maintain balance.   **F**

26. Keep current with the latest technology in order to find even better ways to maximize my flexibility.   **E**

Have a partner, extended family member, or hired help to whom I can delegate activities that don't require my personal involvement.   **C**

IT IS IMPORTANT FOR ME TO:

27.	Engage in activities that meet multiple demands so I can maintain balance among several facets of my life.	D
	Consistently choose to reduce the demands in my life.	F
28.	Arrange my life in cycles: intensive work, followed by intensive personal life, followed by intensive work, and so on.	B
	Use time management techniques to try and do as many work and personal activities as possible.	A
29.	Take full advantage of technology to provide flexibility in order to help me meet the demands of life.	E
	Make fewer commitments in my personal life, but get more out of the things to which I do commit.	D
30.	Delegate responsibilities to willing others when my participation is not required.	C
	Have it all by personally staying involved in all aspects of my work and nonwork life.	A

(Continued)

SCORING

Once you have completed the test, go back through it and add up the number of times you circled each letter. Write the number of times in the space provided below. If you have completed the test accurately up to this point, the grand total will be thirty.

YOUR SCORES:

Juggling   A = 2
Alternating   B = 3
Outsourcing   C = 10

Bundling   D = 4
Techflexing   E = 4
Simplifying   F = 7

For those who prefer a visual representation of their current Balance Strategies Profile, plot your scores on the grid below.

	Juggling	Alternating	Outsourcing	Bundling	Techflexing	Simplifying
10			X			
9			X			
8			X			
7			X			X
6			X			X
5			X			X
4			X	X	X	X
3		X	X	X	X	X
2	X	X	X	X	X	X
1	X	X	X	X	X	X
0	X	X	X	X	X	X

WHAT STRATEGIES BEST FIT YOUR STYLE AND PREFERENCES?

The following worksheet will help you get a clear picture of which strategies you are now using. It will also summarize gaps between where you are now and where you want to be both short term and long term. We will use this worksheet throughout this chapter and the next to compile an integrated rebalancing plan.

Having completed the Balance Strategies Profile (BSP), rank the strategies in order from the highest to lowest score, according to your BSP results.

BALANCE STRATEGIES WORKSHEET

Balance Strategy	Score	Personal Preferences	Current Life Stage	Next Life Stage
1. Outsourcing	10			
2. Simplifying	7			
3. Bundling	4			
4. Tradeoffs	4			
5. Alternating	3			
6. Juggling	2			

EXAMPLE: If your score for juggling was 10 and it was your highest score, you would put "juggling" in row 1 under the Balance Strategy column and "10" under the "Score" column, also on row 1. Then list your next highest strategy and score, and so on. We'll use the rest of the worksheet as we further analyze your current and future strategy options.

As you look over the results of your profile, consider your current use of the various strategies. Take note of all the strategies with a score of "7" or more—they're the ones you rely on to a significant degree. Then ask yourself these questions:

- What's working well when you use those strategies?

- What's not working well?

- How well do the strategies fit the structure and resources of your life right now? For example, if you're currently alternating and it's leaving you exposed financially during the years when you'd rather be focusing on wealth accumulation, there might be other ways to recover from overwork that better meet your needs.

- How well do your current strategies fit your own personal values? Let's say you're fundamentally frugal by nature but find that you rely heavily on outsourcing, which causes you to feel constant anxiety about the money you're paying out for goods and services. You might find it more satisfying to pursue another option.

For additional insight into which strategies are the best fit for you, go back to the aptitude tests at the beginning of chapters 3 through 7. As you review your responses to the self-assessments, think about these questions:

- Which strategies seemed like a good fit for you?

- Which were poor choices, given your personality and style?

- Are there gaps between the strategies that seem to be the best fit for you and your current strategy profile?

The following table gives you a summary of the key issues and requirements for each strategy:

Strategy	Characteristics of Successful Practitioners
JUGGLING	• Enormously high energy • Commitment to "having it all"; unwillingness to give up any of your priorities or delegate them to others • Acceptance of guilty feelings when things fall through the cracks
ALTERNATING	• Ability to earn a lot of money quickly and an accompanying ability to save for times when work is not a priority • A profession that has built-in peaks and valleys • Willingness to take turns with a spouse or partner in the primary breadwinner role • Alternate high and low engagement by looking for assignments of varying intensity
OUTSOURCING	• High income or very supportive, reciprocal network • Ability to manage many resources simultaneously • Willingness to give up personal control of some activities or tasks • Willingness to go "against the norm" in terms of social or peer expectations about what you should do yourself and what you should hire out
BUNDLING	• Strong value and aptitude for efficiency • Good planning and organizing skills • Low need for boundaries; strong desire for integration between the various aspects of your life • Ability to communicate prolifically and keep many people in the loop

Strategy	Characteristics of Successful Practitioners
TECHFLEXING	• Strong technology skills and interest • Profession or role that is conducive to not working face to face • Low need for social interaction at work • Ability to manage professional relationships and networks from a distance • Organization and infrastructure technical support
SIMPLIFYING	• Clear values; ability to align investment of time and money with personal priorities • Willingness to place less emphasis on income and professional status • Willingness to minimize material possessions • Willingness to simplify relationships and manage carefully relationships that are affected by the simplifying strategy

None of this is to say that you ought to change strategies. On the contrary—you are probably adept at using your current choices. So before you opt to change, ask these questions about your current profile:

• How could you use your current strategies more effectively? For example, if you use outsourcing as a dominant strategy, are there more activities you could off-load to your network of suppliers? Or if you're a bundler by nature, can you think of areas in your life where you could multipurpose even more?

• Do your dominant strategies complement each other in ways that could help you? For example, the same ability to delegate that makes outsourcing work might also serve you well in techflexing.

Taking all of these considerations into account, mark an X in the "Personal Preferences" column of the Balance Strategies Worksheet next to the two or three strategies that seem like the best personal fit for you.

CURRENT AND FUTURE LIFE STAGE CONSIDERATIONS

Your efforts to apply one of the five balance strategies, or a combination of them, will be more fruitful if you take into account your current life and career circumstances. In the preceding chapters, we've highlighted the issues of occupational fit, family situation, and even personality as we've discussed the potential compatibility of each strategy with your life and values. The right balance strategy, like the right investment strategy, depends on your personal life and profession. Thinking about your present balance needs, as well as looking toward future life stages, will help you plan how to invest your energy and resources.

Think about your career in three segments—early, mid-, and late. The age boundaries between these segments are not hard and fast; some people are barely starting their careers at age thirty, while others have already been working for ten years. People who have children in their early twenties will face different issues at different times than their childless counterparts or their colleagues who put off having children until later. So focus less on the age per se and more on the issues that apply to your current circumstances.

EARLY CAREER

You're in early career if you

- Are working hard to establish credibility

- Are working hard to establish a nonstudent personal identity

- Feel that you have a reasonably high learning curve at work

Making generalizations about the appropriate balance strategy for early career is difficult, since this may be the stage where lifestyles and responsibilities vary most widely. Many people are working hard to establish both careers and families; others are enjoying the freedom of having less structure and more money than in their student years. As economic demands increase and social norms trend toward putting off marriage and children (or foregoing them altogether), the balance strategies appropriate for the emerging generation are evolving. Given what we know now, however, here's a look at how the five strategies might be applied during this life stage.

First, it's worth considering whether work-life balance is the right goal at this point in your career. Throwing yourself into your work is a normal, even helpful, part of establishing a professional identify and laying a foundation for your whole career. In addition, it can help you pay off student loans. "The craziest time of my life was right after I graduated from college," says Nicole Abbott, a retail manager in St. Louis. "I was the assistant manager of a store, and my job was to stay up until 4:00 A.M. for display changes, then be back at 9:00 A.M. to open. For about two years, all I did was work and sleep (although looking back, I don't remember the sleep). But I knew it wasn't forever. I kept it up just long enough to get out of debt, then I quit." Most research on life stage development suggests that establishing a strong personal identity in early career is very important;[2] building a foundation of competency and the beginnings of a professional track record may give you more options when life gets more complicated in midcareer.

Despite the need to establish credibility in early career, some people may postpone the official start of their careers by trying many different jobs before settling on their first long-term professional commitment. Alternating works well in early career for those who manage to minimize their commitments or who agree on long-term compromises with a partner. The premortgage years may provide the financial flexibility to take extended breaks from work, providing an opportunity to sample a broad range of long-term options. The lack of childcare or elder-care responsibilities can add to the sense of freedom. Although financial planners warn against waiting until midcareer to start building a nest egg, those who are willing to focus on autonomy rather than their retirement account may find that alternating buys them balance, while also allowing them to establish a reputation for hard work and focus.

After graduation from college, Emily Jacobs interned in Washington with a senator from her home state. Six months later, she traveled to China and spent half a year teaching English part-time and studying Mandarin—more of an extended vacation than a job. She returned to her parents' home in the Midwest, and spent a year working for the National Park Service. After another three-month travel break to see all of the states in the United States she had never visited before, she accepted a Peace Corps assignment in Paraguay, where she developed a number of nutrition training programs for the residents of several rural communities. When she returned to the United States, she worked as a museum guide in Philadelphia, providing tours in Spanish for Hispanic school children.

When she was twenty-eight, just as her parents were beginning to warn that she needed to establish a career and a stable life, Emily met and married her husband, Mark, who was just finishing a masters of business administration program at the Wharton School. He accepted a job with a large computer manufacturer in Phoenix. Although she didn't have any specific credentials for the job, Emily found work as a technical trainer with the same company; her new employer was impressed by her presentation skills and her ability to master a vast array of challenging situations. After a few months, Emily was working just as intensively as Mark. The couple expects that they will take turns in the lead breadwinner role over time, although both may need to be more career focused during the years of saving for college tuition for their children or for retirement, especially given their late start at savings.

Juggling is often a necessity in early career, especially for people who are paying their professional dues. The first ten years beyond school are usually the ideal time to establish a professional reputation and to build up the kind of credibility that may allow for more flexibility and a higher income later on. It's also the traditional time for marrying and starting to have children—another huge time commitment that often competes with professional demands. Failure to capitalize on either opportunity during this period may preclude them later on. Starting a career with a company once you've reached midlife means opting off an upwardly mobile career path and may even limit employability, given today's competitive environment. Midlife also means a shrinking pool of eligible partners, waning energy, and, particularly for women, diminishing fertility, all of which combine to make child rearing less likely or less attractive after the mid-to-late thirties.

As long as it's seen as a short-term strategy, juggling can allow individuals to maintain an acceptable level of balance as a bridge to a life stage where competing demands subside or become more easily managed. When career credibility is established or when children are old enough to be comparatively self-sufficient, juggling can be replaced by another strategy.

Outsourcing is probably a less viable option in early career, given that these are the lowest income years. Our research indicates that those who identified outsourcing as a primary strategy tend to be older than those who use the other strategies—a logical finding based on typical income levels. Young careerists who opt to use outsourcing to gain greater balance should generally hire others to do one or two high-priority, time-consuming tasks. As an alternative, they may explore outsourcing options that are not financial transactions, such as babysitting co-ops or service exchanges.

The characteristics of early career that make it a poor match for outsourcing make it an excellent time to simplify. If you can maintain some of the elements of simplicity that likely got you through your prepaycheck years, you can avoid having to scale back dramatically if you adopt this strategy later on.

Techflexing and bundling are appropriate strategies at any career stage. One caveat is that techflexing usually requires establishing enough credibility and trust that your employer is willing to grant you a flexible work arrangement. Bundling in early career may provide valuable practice for continuing the strategy in midcareer, when life often becomes more complex and there are more variables to manage.

MIDCAREER

By midcareer, you've established your professional credibility, you work independently or even in formal or informal leadership roles. On the home front, you have settled into a long-term relationship or have established other consistent personal patterns. These are demanding years on all fronts. For those who had children when they were in their late twenties to midthirties, midcareer is the time when their family demands are the heaviest. On the work side, most people have established a solid reputation by the age of thirty-five, setting up their midcareer years as the period when they make their most significant professional contributions. And because these are prime earning years for both retirement savings and for children's college funds, succeeding on the job is critical from a financial perspective.

Most people in this phase of life also have the desire and ability to pursue nonwork, nonfamily interests such as volunteering, hobbies, or physical fitness. There may be a growing recognition that energy and physical stamina will decline with age and an accompanying desire to avoid putting off those pursuits until retirement. For these reasons, a change in balance strategy may be in order during these years.

Juggling may have outlived its usefulness by midcareer. As energy tapers off and demands increase, those who could juggle their way through anything in early career may find that continuing to sacrifice sleep, while compromising on almost all of their personal priorities, may begin to take a toll on their health, their creativity, and their zest for life. The proverbial midlife reevaluation of priorities and direction helps many people recognize the high price exacted by juggling and drives them to focus their efforts on their highest priorities. This may facilitate a good deal of simplifying, as midcareerists begin narrowing down the list of activities and people that they want to invest in. Simplifying also often increases as professionals clarify their internal career values and their personal criteria for success.

Outsourcing may also be a viable strategy as jugglers become more focused on what's important to them. Midcareer professionals often have the resources to hire out more responsibilities. Increasing family demands, such as children or aging parents, may require outsourcing to some degree, particularly for single or divorced professionals or two-career couples.

Techflexing, an acceptable strategy in early career, may become even more viable in midcareer. Experienced professionals may have the credibility and influence to negotiate more flexibility, such as working from home either full time or part time. They may also have enough seasoned perspective to make significant contributions from remote locations. Techflexing might not work as well for individuals for whom face-to-face contact with colleagues, direct reports, or customers remains critical (managers or salespeople, for example). However, even in these cases, technology may be used to build in schedule flexibility while still maintaining open lines of communication. Some managers have discovered that being available electronically after the end of the formal workday can buy them some freedom between 9:00 A.M. and 5:00 P.M.

Mario Gomez is a senior level manager who has used technology to smooth over some of the challenges that come in midcareer. Mario's wife also has a demanding career, and they work hard to parent equally. Mario's company places an unusually high value on time spent in the office, and he recognizes the risk in ducking out early to carpool or go to a Little League game. Nevertheless, he also has an agreement with his wife that they will cover for each other, allowing each to stay late at the office two nights per week. So he uses a collection of electronic tools to help him cover all of the bases. In a memo to his staff, he provides explicit detail about how to get in touch with him at what times of day—if his cell phone is turned off during dinner, for example, they're welcome to page him. If it's an emergency, they should start the page with "911" before leaving a more detailed message. He also lets his staff know that he'll log onto e-mail after his daughters are in bed. Mario's colleagues and his wife joke that his cell phone has grown into his skull—but the technology gives him a way to figuratively be in more than one place at a time.

Alternating may be less useful in midcareer than in early or late career, at least for primary breadwinners. Financial stability becomes more important, and alternating without a backup can create too much financial risk. Most people see these years as the primary period for wealth accumulation, and with increasing uncertainty about traditional retirement income sources, financial stability becomes more important. Some midcareer professionals find that they can continue to alternate if their jobs enable it or if they have a spouse or partner who is willing and able to trade off breadwinner responsibilities with them. Alternating may also work on a small scale, such as negotiating a consolidated work schedule or actively taking advantage of occasional slow periods. Other midcareer alternating options, particularly for those whose family demands increase during this period, include job sharing or working part time—as long as you can still make ends meet.

Bundling works well at this stage and becomes more important as the number of competing demands increases for most people. Former jugglers often find bundling an efficient alternative. Both juggling and bundling appeal to similar balancing needs (maintaining commitments on all fronts), with similar compromises (not pursuing any one priority to its fullest).

LATE CAREER

This life stage is defined by some or all of the following characteristics:

- You are within ten to fifteen years of retirement.

- If you have children, they are no longer living at home and you no longer support them financially.

- You have established yourself in a profession, industry, or company.

Given these characteristics, here are some of the implications for each of the work-life balance strategies:

Juggling. If you're still doing this, either you really enjoy it or it's time to stop. Your energy levels aren't what they once were. You don't need the added stress.

Simplifying. This strategy makes more and more sense for people as they near retirement. If your nest is now empty, by definition your life is simpler. In addition, many people prepare for retirement by streamlining their lives and focusing on what's most important to them. "How do I really want to spend my remaining productive years?" is a question worth asking. Don't be surprised if the answer leads to some significant simplifying in your social life, your home environment, and even your on-the-job activities.

Alternating. Depending on your financial situation, your later years can be an ideal time to implement this strategy. Suppose you have a significant nest egg, a home that has appreciated substantially, or generous guaranteed retirement benefits—or all three. While you don't necessarily want or need to work full time anymore, the idea of nonstop gardening, fishing, traveling, or golfing doesn't sound that great, either. Alternating can be the best choice if you want to stay involved in your profession post-retirement.

Rick Wilkins spent a productive thirty-year career as an engineer and manager for a large chemical company. At the age of fifty-seven, he took early retirement. "The company was downsizing, and the package they offered was too good to pass up," he says. His three kids were all grown, raising families of their own. He and his wife had built a summer home outside of Jackson, Wyoming. He could have easily slipped into a life of leisure—but he didn't want to.

Instead, he linked up with a consulting firm that uses him now and then as a contractor. When he's in the middle of a project, the work is intense. But projects rarely last more than a month or two, allowing him to go back to full-time moose-watching and grandparenting until the next project. For Rick, it's an ideal mix.

"I love the freedom to travel around the country and visit my kids and grandkids," he says, "but I also love my work. It gives me some intellectual stimulation—and it gets me out of the house once in a while, which I think my wife appreciates."

A similar approach will work preretirement if you're able to negotiate a job-sharing, part-time, or flextime arrangement with your employer. If your financial commitments will not allow such a move, consider one of the remaining strategies.

Techflexing. This strategy can work at any age and life stage. The main criterion is professional fit. One mitigating factor is that many people have moved into managerial roles by late career, and techflexing doesn't lend itself to hands-on people management. But don't eliminate the possibility. The summer before he retired, Rick Wilkins talked his boss into letting him telecommute from his Wyoming home to the Michigan office. He was doing project work at the time—"the kind of thing I could do from anywhere," he says. "It gave me a great opportunity to test the waters and see if I could work effectively outside the corporate environment."

Outsourcing. This is an ideal strategy for many late-career balance seekers. With a decent income and no kids at home, they can afford more of the services that seemed unjustifiable luxuries before. Many people at this point in their lives feel they deserve a little pampering. Moving to a condominium, leasing a car, eating out more often—all of these become more feasible (and, the demographic studies show, more typical) in late career.

Bundling. Of all the strategies for balance, this one is the least age- or stage-dependent. It always works. But with the children out of the house, you may feel less of an imperative to bundle. Work-family integration just isn't as complicated anymore. In fact, you may have the opposite challenge: a life spent multipurposing creates habits that are hard to break. If you're getting tired of trying to pack extra meaning into every activity, relax and do one thing at a time. It's a small indulgence, but you've earned it.

COMPLETING YOUR BALANCE STRATEGIES WORKSHEET

Considering your current and future life stages is important because your work life and your personal life may both change in three to five years. You may need to make some lifestyle or job-style changes soon in order to reach your long-term goal. For example, investing in continuing education for your partner now might allow you more career flexibility in a few years.

Now go back to the Balance Strategies Worksheet (on page 167). In the column labeled "Current Life Stage," put an X next to the balance strategies that seem most appropriate for your current career situation. If you're not nearing retirement, do the same thing for the life stage you're approaching.

Perhaps such an extensive approach to analyzing one's work-life balance seems a little ironic. After all, aren't we trying to get away from overscheduling? Yet the experience of the last thirty years shows that wishing and waiting won't make balance happen. As Rahm Emanuel, a senior advisor for policy and strategy in the Clinton administration put it, "You've got to be as determined in your personal life as you are in your professional life."[3]

In this chapter, you've analyzed your own approach to work-life balance and established a profile for what works well and what doesn't. Completing this process involves examining your current strategies and putting them in the context of your personality, values, and life stage. In the next chapter, we'll apply your profile to create a rebalancing plan.

10

Rebalance Your Life

"MY KIDS HAVE a picture book called *The Pancake King*. It's about this boy who has a passion for making pancakes. Pretty soon he's lured into going commercial and is producing so many pancakes so fast that he no longer enjoys it. I've often thought that the book is a perfect metaphor for my life," explained a public accountant and father of four in Mission Viejo, California. "I'm the boy in the chef's hat, holding a spatula. The griddle's at least a hundred yards long. People keep pouring batter on the griddle, and I'm running the length of it trying to flip the pancakes before they burn to a crisp. I end up with a lot of charred pancakes."

Rebalancing may require small or large changes in perspective, practices, or values. Approaching it unsystematically has helped us get where we are today—a nation of jugglers. Now you know which strategies you've been using, and you've thought about how well they're working. You've considered the strategies in light of your personality and your current and future life stages. In this chapter, we'll talk about turning that insight into action that will help you burn fewer pancakes, so to speak.

HOW MUCH BALANCE, REALLY?

The first question is, How much do you really want to rebalance your life? Our research shows that 40 percent of professionals in large companies value work-life balance over other career drivers, and many more than that have it as a secondary or back-up driver. Even among careerists who value advancement, challenge, freedom, or security the most, maintaining some level of balance may become necessary to foster healthy relationships outside of work. After completing Derr's Career Orientations Self-Assessment, one workshop participant concluded: "When I completed the assessment the way I really feel, the most important driver for me was freedom. When I completed it the way I thought my wife would want me to, balance came out the highest."[1]

If you've made it to this point in this book, chances are you feel significant internal or external motivation to achieve a better balance. However, our years of work on career development issues in large organizations have shown that it's becoming politically correct to claim balance as your primary goal. Balance has become a popular measure of true success, with free time the ultimate status symbol. Ted Turner loves talking about the amount of time he spends on his ranch, and Jack Welch openly admits to indulging his passion for golf. If your efforts to rebalance are born mostly of external expectations that aren't deeply rooted in your own feelings and beliefs, you may find your motivation somewhat limited.

Like any significant life change, rebalancing won't be effective if you don't believe that it's necessary and important—even if your value for rebalancing comes indirectly because a lack of balance is threatening key relationships in your life. Rebalancing requires making changes in the way you think about life and in the way you behave. It requires learning new skills and, in some cases, developing new types of relationships. Our lives didn't easily get out of balance; numerous forces are pulling on us to keep them out of alignment. An equal and opposing commitment is required to be in balance more often than we are out of it.

One key to deciding how much balance you want is to think about how you're going to use those extra hours. Free time isn't worth much unless you know where to spend it. Answer the following questions to assess your commitment to real change:

- Of the three main areas in your life—your work, your relationships, and your personal care and development—where do you want to focus more of your time and attention?

- What will give you the greatest sense of well-being?

- Which is suffering most—your work, your personal life, or your relationships?

- Which area is your highest priority?

To some extent, creating a balance plan is akin to creating a budget for your finances. With the exception of the fanatically frugal, most people find it much easier to save money when they have a goal in mind, whether it be saving for a major event (new car, college tuition, or retirement) or to get out of debt. In the same way, rebalancing can free you up for activities you wish you had time for (hobbies, friendships, or exercise). Or it may be a way to take care of some of life's necessities that you're currently ignoring—a way of making up a "balance deficit"—by spending more time on fundamentals such as raising your children, mowing the lawn, or sleeping. In either case, a plan for rebalancing can reduce your stress level and increase your enjoyment. If you don't have a specific target, you may find that work expands to fill any possible gains in free time. Or you may find that the work it takes to rebalance isn't worthwhile if you devote your time savings to watching hours of MTV or mindlessly surfing the Internet (unless that's what really brings you fulfillment).

This leads us to our next questions:

- What is rebalancing going to buy you?

- What's your overall objective in rebalancing?

It's important to be clear about these fundamental questions. They will provide direction and focus for the rest of your plan. Assuming that either internal values or external pressures have raised your motivation for change to a critical level, the following techniques and tools can help you rebalance. They'll also help you complete your plan.

CHOOSING A STRATEGY

The first step in creating your rebalancing plan is to focus on one or two strategies that you want to emphasize. Your Balance Strategy Worksheet should be helpful here. Go back and look at the boxes you marked under each of the columns. Use the worksheet to answer these questions:

- How well aligned are the strategies you marked in the Score column and those you checked in the Personal Preferences column? Does this support your impressions about your current ability to achieve balance? Does it highlight obvious opportunities for change?

- If there is a lot of variance between the two columns, are you interested in and committed to resolving the differences?

- How aligned are the strategies you marked in the Score column and those you identified in the Current Life Stage column? Is this consistent with your impressions about your current ability to achieve balance? Does it highlight additional opportunities for change?

- Are the strategies you marked in the Personal Preferences column aligned with those in the Current Life Stage column? If not, how much are you willing to compromise? Is it more important to you to stay within your comfort zone or to do something that might be a better fit for your life situation?

- How aligned are your Score and Next Life Stage columns? Do you want to plan for major modifications in anticipation of the next stage? If so, which strategies will make the most sense a few years from now? How do those strategies fit with your personal preferences?

Answering these questions should help you identify one or two strategies to work on right away and possibly one or two others to focus on a couple of years down the road.

BUILDING YOUR INFRASTRUCTURE

In the physical world, infrastructure describes the basic facilities and improvements that undergird civilization: roadways, railways, electric power, telephone lines, banking regulations, the legal system, and so forth. Your personal career infrastructure lays a foundation for your choices around work-life balance. Its components include demonstrating your technical competence on the job, working long and hard when necessary to show commitment, paying your dues at the entry level, internalizing the company culture, and building a network of supportive peers. These career basics help make you a valued resource, someone the company wants to retain. Infrastructure is equally important in your nonwork life. Would living closer to family give you more support and more options? Have you created a network of friends with similar interests and concerns? Do you have a handle on your personal finances to the point that you know how flexible you can afford to be? Answers to these kinds of questions will provide a solid base for any of the balance strategies. The following table provides some ideas about what type of infrastructure you might want to build for each of the balance strategies.

Strategy	Helpful Infrastructure
JUGGLING	• Strong support networks • Understanding spouse, partner, or significant others • Willingness to pay dues
ALTERNATING	• Significant educational investment in order to maximize your earning potential • Significant financial reserves • Strong professional skills and reputation
OUTSOURCING	• Substantial income • Strong referral network • Backup resources for key suppliers
BUNDLING	• Close alignment between personal and professional demands and interest, e.g., geographic location is the same • Backup resources when complex plans go awry
TECHFLEXING	• Access to the right equipment • Organizational support for telecommuting • Demonstrated ability to work remotely • Internalizing the company culture
SIMPLIFYING	• Sustainable low-cost lifestyle • Support of family or significant others • Strong professional skills and reputation

Some infrastructure requirements will help regardless of your chosen strategy—for example, having a strong professional reputation can never be a liability. However, it's more critical to some strategies than others. The point here is to identify the elements that are critical given where you want to go and to make building them a part of your plan if they don't exist already. Try answering these questions:

- What skills, abilities, or resources would help you rebalance, given the short-term strategy you've chosen? What do you need to do to build them into your portfolio?

- How will your infrastructure needs be different in a few years, when you reach the next life stage? What can you start doing now to prepare so that you'll be ready to switch strategies, if necessary?

LETTING GO

Successful balancers learn to relinquish control. They delegate. Letting go—of having to do it all themselves, of certain societal conventions and expectations, of traditional proprieties—can be enormously liberating. The best balancers don't abandon their values; they just stop living their lives according to someone else's definition of success. So if you've been clawing your way up the management ladder because you know it would make your mother (spouse, neighbors, in-laws) proud—yet you currently enjoy your work and earn enough to meet or exceed your economic needs—think about some alternatives.

"I got to the point where I was aiming for a big management job, when I realized that I would probably hate that kind of work," an engineer in a research laboratory told us. "It was a big relief to realize that I would be a lot happier if I focused on what would bring me joy—the science part of the job—instead of trying to fit someone else's definition of success." If you were raised to believe that only snobs have hired household help, but have discovered by now that you could easily live without the money it would cost to hire a cleaning service, and feel you can trust someone else to effectively scrub the bathtub, trade some money for a little more free time. To identify what you could let go of, consider the following questions:

- What tasks can you give up completely?

- What tasks can you delegate to someone else?

- What attitudes or values do you need to change in order to implement your chosen strategy? Do you need to change the way you've been defining career success? We're not suggesting that you compromise your integrity. We're just encouraging you to question some assumptions that might be getting in the way of rebalancing.

- What expectations do others have of you that you will need to deal with in order to implement your chosen strategy? Key others might include your manager, your colleagues, your parents, friends, and family.

- What possessions can you eliminate in order to reduce maintenance time or expense? What relationships can you invest less in? (Remember, a little simplifying goes a long way.)

PUTTING IT ALL TOGETHER

You'll make more progress faster if you organize your thoughts on paper. The following plan will help you integrate all of the thinking you've done so far in this chapter. Fill it out or download an electronic copy at www.beyondjuggling.com.

MY REBALANCING PLAN

WHY I WANT TO REBALANCE
Key drivers behind my desire to rebalance:

What I plan to do with the time I accrue by rebalancing:

MY CURRENT AND FUTURE REBALANCING STRATEGIES
My current rebalancing strategies:

Why these strategies work or don't work, given my personal preferences and current career and life circumstances:

The rebalancing strategy I want to emphasize for the time being:

The rebalancing strategy that will work best for my next life stage:

MY CURRENT AND FUTURE INFRASTRUCTURE NEEDS
The resources and capabilities I need to implement my current strategy:

(Continued)

Key resources and capabilities I am currently lacking, and how I plan to develop them:

The resources and capabilities I need to implement my future strategy:

My plan to prepare for the next career stage by building the resources and capabilities I lack now:

MY PLAN TO LET GO
Tasks that I can completely eliminate:

Tasks that I can outsource or delegate to others:

Attitudes or values to let go of:

Expectations of others that affect me and my plan for dealing with them:

Time-consuming possessions or relationships that bring little value to me and my plan for reducing my investment in them:

Once you've planned how you'll approach rebalancing, it's time to create specific ideas for how you'll implement the strategies you've chosen. These ideas should fall into two categories: small changes and large changes. You should focus on small changes in two circumstances. First, there may be little adjustments that will help you significantly improve your balance. Second, your life may be only moderately out of balance in the first place. If that's true, you probably don't need a major overhaul, just a minor tune-up. The table below summarizes the ideas we included at the end of each chapter for small-scale implementation of each strategy.

Strategy	Ideas for Small-Scale Implementation
JUGGLING	• Use as a short-term solution when other strategies fail. • Look for ways to eliminate or reduce it.
ALTERNATING	• Negotiate compensation/free-time trade-offs. • Look for occasional, less intensive assignments. • Look for natural shifts in intensity, such as seasonal breaks or slow periods, and take advantage of those breaks to recharge or regroup. • Use all of your vacation time. • Negotiate a four-day work week or other flexible arrangement.
OUTSOURCING	• Take advantage of gift wrapping or delivery services when you buy items on-line or through a catalog. • Buy convenience foods at the grocery store. • Hire someone to do the household chore you most dislike.

(Continued)

OUTSOURCING *(continued)*	• Try to expand the services you buy from a single provider. For example, if you hire a lawn service, see if they will also weed your flower beds or remove snow during the winter.
BUNDLING	• Plan trips to run errands more carefully so that you can accomplish as much as possible with one trip. • Look for ways to create social opportunities out of everyday tasks or obligations. • Find ways to integrate work responsibilities with other tasks—extend a business trip by a day or two to visit friends or family, or integrate your hobbies and other interests at work.
TECHFLEXING	• If you have a long commute, get a cell phone with a hands-free device. Use it to catch up with friends and family when you're on the road. • If you have access to a laptop computer at work, manage your schedule so that you leave early and finish your on-line work at home, at your own convenience. • If you travel a lot for work, get a personal Internet service provider program installed on your laptop so that you can keep in touch with family and friends while you're traveling. • Do your personal and gift shopping on-line. • Use the Internet to make travel reservations, buy tickets for movies or other entertainment events, or check in for flights. • Distribute your cell phone number to appropriate friends and family so that they can call you easily, no matter where you are.

TECHFLEXING *(continued)*	• Get a pager so that your child or your child's school can get in touch with you at any time. • Take advantage of on-line banking or move to a financial management company that provides the means to track all of your accounts on a single Web site.
SIMPLIFYING	• Minimize business travel. • Pay your bills electronically. • Get more out of your possessions—repair items instead of replacing them, buy a few high quality clothes, and wear them longer. • Say no to volunteer or social opportunities that don't provide the highest value for you. • Focus on the highest impact areas at work; strive to make more of a difference in less time. • Clarify limits with your coworkers; let them know when you won't be available (late at night, weekends) in order to minimize requests that you have to turn down. • Adopt more simple, less-expensive hobbies (e.g., walking versus golf). • Simplify your entertainment and holiday celebrations.

Look through this list and mark any ideas that you could easily adopt, that would liberate even a little bit of time. Or generate your own list of small-scale change ideas for your current and long-term strategies.

PLANNING LARGE-SCALE CHANGE

In some cases, small changes may not be enough. There may be a significant gap between your current strategies and your personal preferences, for example. Or you may be heading for a major career transition that will require a fundamental strategy shift. It's also possible that your life is now seriously out of balance, a desperate situation that calls for more drastic measures. Or your career may simply lack the infrastructure needed to effectively use your current strategy. To make dramatic changes in some aspect of your life requires commitment, planning, and discipline. It also will demand serious introspection and self-evaluation; the changes required to implement it will doubtless also be more emotionally charged. The timelines for putting this type of plan in place will be much longer. The following table will give you some ideas on large-scale changes that will help you make a more significant strategy shift. (You'll notice we've left juggling off the list.)

Strategy	Ideas for Large-Scale Implementation
ALTERNATING	• Change to a profession that has natural peaks and valleys. • Save enough money so that you can take a sabbatical or leave of absence. • Switch to part-time work or a more flexible job role. • Move to an organization that provides a bigger variety of roles or assignments for your profession. • Work for a larger, older organization instead of a smaller, younger company.
OUTSOURCING	• Hire a full-time nanny or other household professional. • Move to a higher paying profession or organization so that you can afford to buy more services. • Hire someone to do something that you previously believed was important to do yourself, e.g., organize your finances or your social life.

BUNDLING	• Change jobs or renegotiate your role so that your personal and work interests are more closely aligned.
	• Move to another house or city so that you are closer to friends or family, or so that additional professional or recreational opportunities are readily available.
	• Negotiate additional resources or flexibility at work so that you can more easily integrate various aspects of your life.
TECHFLEXING	• Create a Web site as a way of keeping in touch with friends and family.
	• Set up a home office.
	• Negotiate an agreement with your manager or department to telecommute full time or part time.
	• Get the training you need to be technologically self-sufficient.
	• Move to a role or organization where telecommuting is more feasible or acceptable.
SIMPLIFYING	• Move closer to your work, or work from home.
	• Find a less demanding job or profession.
	• Look for roles at work where you can work more independently, and where other people don't rely on you for day-to-day direction or support.
	• Turn down promotions or intense projects that don't give you the balance you need.
	• Decide which relationships are the most important in your life. Invest in them, and spend less time with friends or associates who bring less value to your life.
	• Landscape your yard so that it requires less maintenance.

Read through the list of large-scale changes to see if any of them make sense, given the strategies you have chosen to pursue. Other necessary changes may occur to you that are not on this list. For any large-scale changes that you plan, ask yourself the following questions:

- Are you committed enough to this change to make it work? Is it realistic?

- How will the people in your life who are affected by these changes react to them? What is your plan for winning their support?

- How will this change affect you financially? What is your plan for dealing with major expenses or reductions in income?

- How long will it take you to implement the change?

- How will the changes affect your long-term career opportunities? Can you make the change and still achieve career success, however you define it?

Complete the following boxes as the last step in your plan.

MY REBALANCING PLAN, CONTINUED

SMALL-SCALE CHANGES I PLAN TO MAKE (with Target Dates):
Alternating:

Outsourcing:

Bundling:

Techflexing:

Simplifying:

LARGE-SCALE CHANGES I PLAN TO MAKE:
Specific changes:

Strategy or strategies I will use to implement the changes:

Obstacles I will need to overcome or address:

My plan for addressing those obstacles:

Congratulations! You've finished your plan. Now the real work begins.

IMPLEMENTING YOUR PLAN

One of the first steps in implementing your plan is to share it with someone else—your manager or mentor, your spouse or partner, a close friend, or a colleague who is also working to rebalance. Sharing your plan will accomplish several objectives beyond a reality check on whether or not it's feasible. You'll increase your commitment to making it happen, and you'll have someone to hold you accountable for achieving the goals you've set.

You can get support from other people who might be affected by your plan. Finally, by talking it over, you'll identify inconsistencies or gaps in the plan. The best way to share your plan is in a face-to-face meeting—you'll benefit from much more input and helpful feedback. If that's not possible, exchange it by e-mail, or talk it through over the phone.

Even with a supportive network of family and friends, however, implementing the plan is all up to you. The balance strategies put rebalancing within your control. Luckily, the rewards are automatic and self-reinforcing. Keep the following tips in mind as you attempt to increase your satisfaction by getting beyond juggling:

- Establish milestones and celebrate your achievement of them.

- Experiment and adjust the plan as you go along; it's intended as a starting place to help give you direction and focus.

- Exchange ideas and progress reports with others.

- Review your plan frequently in order to keep it fresh and in focus.

A FINAL WORD

In our research, we never came across a self-described "perfectly balanced" person. Perhaps this is just as well. Human beings achieve a state of continual equilibrium only in death—and not even the most harried juggler is anxious for that type of balance. As Woody Allen put it, "I don't fear death. I just don't want to be there when it happens." No matter how crazy, hectic, or out of control life gets, it sure beats the alternative.

So in a world overflowing with meaningful opportunities and fascinating distractions, work-life balance will always be a challenge. We've tried to share with you a simple, structured approach to the complicated, dynamic process we call rebalancing. Our hope is that you will adopt something—an idea, a framework, an example— that helps you get beyond juggling on the journey to a richer, more satisfying life.

APPENDIX: HOW MANAGERS CAN USE THIS BOOK

ALTHOUGH THE FOCUS of this book has been on the individual, work-life balance is also a vital organizational issue. In the management of talent, a sensible work-life philosophy and support system can dramatically increase retention, creating strong bonds between an employee and a company. In addition, workers who are less burned out tend to be more productive and creative. Management guru Dave Ulrich points out that having both a meaningful life and meaningful work is a key intrinsic human motivator.[1]

For many years, work-life balance was a taboo topic in corporate America. Managers expected their employees to demonstrate ambition, dedication, and "fire in the belly." This often meant making personal and/or family sacrifices to put the company first. Today, work-life balance is at least a talking point on most employers' human resources agendas. This represents tremendous progress. To borrow economist Albert Hirschman's useful "exit, voice, and loyalty" terminology, work-life tension has long existed but was handled primarily via "loyalty"—employees suffered in silence, not wanting their personal lives to cost them on-the-job advancement. Work-life issues are now a matter of "voice"—a legitimate point of discussion and negotiation between employee and employer. Well-managed companies try to avoid letting work-life frustration become the reason talented employees leave the company—the final option, termed "exit" by Hirschman.[2]

The ideas and concepts presented in this book can be applied as tools for effective human resource management, coaching, and training. Specific application ideas, including an outline for a simple work-life balance workshop or brown-bag seminar, can be found at www.beyondjuggling.com. Following are tips for managers who want to increase the motivation and loyalty of their balance-seeking employees.

TIPS FOR MANAGING JUGGLERS

Since juggling is the default strategy, most managers already know what it's like to oversee jugglers. They know the jugglers' energy and efficiency, their desire for flexibility, and their dislike for participating where they are not needed. Managers may also have seen over time the burn-out that often accompanies juggling. Here are a few ideas that may help as they work with their large contingent of jugglers; the ideas are applicable to other balance seekers as well.

1. *Offer career- and life-planning workshops.* Managers should understand that juggling, successful or not, stems from a sincere desire for work-life balance. Helping the employee attain that balance is to the advantage of both employer and employee. Jugglers want it all, need it all to be happy, and are willing to work very hard to have it all. They have a genuine commitment to their work. In addition, if they can arrive at a balancing configuration that works, they will be loyal to the company that helps them perpetuate it. Offering seminars that delineate possible career strategies is one of the best ways to help jugglers decide if balance truly is their dominant career driver and how they can best realize it.

2. *Help them consider other strategies.* Since juggling often is not a wise long-term strategy, help the worker consider other balancing strategies: outsourcing, techflexing, alternating, or bundling. Outsourcing is one of the best alternate strategies for jugglers. They will still do all of the most important things themselves, and the second-most important things will still get done, just not by them.

3. *Respect their time.* What is a good idea for all workers is absolutely crucial for jugglers. An experienced employee who is juggling probably knows the amount of time she needs to complete a given assignment, and she is more than willing to give it. Requiring her presence at meetings where she is only marginally needed will frustrate her. Tasks and meetings that pop up unexpectedly will likewise disrupt her juggling act. Give her enough lead time that she can arrange other aspects of her life to fit.

4. *Look for ways to be more flexible.* Sometimes emergencies do arise, both at work and at home. Jugglers will be willing to meet a company crisis or contribute extra hours in an emergency especially if the company is willing to give them extra accommodation when crises develop in the other arenas of their lives. In fact, most jugglers really can't function long-term without options when they need them. Todd Sterling (introduced in chapter 2) knows that if he needs to, he can work from home for an afternoon or a day. During soccer season, he'll want to leave on time to make it to practice. But he will also work late into the night after his children are in bed and come into the office early the next morning when a high-stakes deal is near closing.

5. *Find ways to make some self-care services available.* Since jugglers most often skimp on their own self-care and personal development, make it easier for them by offering some at work.

Sponsor a lunch-time exercise group. Bring in a massage therapist. Just asking your employees what rejuvenates them will help both of you. They will be reminded to take care of themselves, and you may learn if they are close to burn-out before it's too late to prevent it.

6. *Provide time-management resources.* If it fits within your budget and policy constraints, provide Palm Pilots, planners, cell phones, or quieter workspaces. Jugglers are far happier when they can maximize their efficiency. Ask them what will help them. If given the resources to do so, they will almost always provide high-quality, creative, and dependable work within the agreed time schedule.

7. *Provide other on-site services.* Jill Blackham, a juggler and manager of organizational effectiveness at Cisco (see chapter 2), recommends that all companies take better care of their employees by providing on-site childcare; offering long sabbaticals so that employees can recharge; and implementing a wide variety of job-rotation, job-sharing, and other flexible arrangements. Doing so will "support people who want balance in their lives without forcing them to quit or sacrifice everything for work. It will pay off for the company in increased productivity and employee effectiveness," she argues. Employees at K-Mart's headquarters, for example, can take home specially prepared turkey-with-all-the-fixings meals at holiday time. It's a small gesture but it helps reduce the stress during a high-pressure season of the year.

8. *Send them home.* You probably know your staff well enough to notice when someone is staying late for no real reason. A simple, "Hey, why don't you get out of here?" can be just what the doctor ordered. You'll get more work out of a recovered juggler than a burned-out one. And as difficult as it is to do, examine your own behavior to determine if you are exacerbating the jug-

gler's problem. Because they are typically capable and efficient, successful jugglers may be the first people you think of when handing out new assignments. Be careful not to overassign.

TIPS FOR MANAGING ALTERNATERS

If you manage individuals who use an alternating strategy, there's a lot you can do to help them get the balance they need while also keeping them engaged in the organization. The long-term payoff is higher productivity on the job, as well as keeping good people who might otherwise leave.

1. *Provide flexibility and variety in assignments.* Most people who choose alternating as a primary strategy also like variety in the type of assignments they are given. That variety may include differences in the substance of the assignment (line versus staff, many different types of projects, and so forth). More importantly, managers can pay attention to the intensity of projects. If an alternater has been at the top of the stress scale for the last three years, think about an assignment that suits her skills but taxes her less for a few months.

2. *Don't view a request for less intensity as a personal affront.* It's easy to talk about accommodating varying commitment levels in the abstract, but having someone opt out of your work group—either full time or part time—can feel like a personal betrayal when managers think about the amount of work left uncovered by a reduction in experienced resources. Working past the initial emotional reaction might just lead to a new arrangement that will keep both parties happy for the long term.

3. *Recognize that it may be better to keep a top performer part time than to lose him full time.* Alternating will always raise concerns about an individual's ability to contribute. Will key customers

still buy from us if this is the person who has the key relationship with them? Can someone really be an effective manager if
he's here only three days a week? Will it frustrate this person's
internal clients if she isn't in the office to take phone calls all day,
every day? A willingness to experiment with approaches such as
flextime, telecommuting, sabbaticals, or leaves of absence, will
often show that even if some concerns are warranted, the overall cost to the organization will be less by accommodating the
alternater than by losing her. Remember Jane Elmore's experience (chapter 3). She took three unpaid leaves from her consulting firm—maternity leave with each of her two children plus
a six-month tour of Asia to celebrate her husband's graduation
from medical school. "I worried a lot about asking for the first
leave for the trip to Asia," Jane says. "My boss didn't hesitate to
give me the time, even though it meant having to restaff a large
project. When I asked him later why he'd been so accommodating, he said that he thought it was better to give me six months
off than to have me quit altogether. He was right—I had decided
to quit if it meant not being able to take time off. When they
supported me, it earned my loyalty for seven more years."

4. *Look for ways to keep alternaters in the loop during their periods of reduced engagement.* Maintaining the relationships that
   could dwindle during downtimes works better if it works both
   ways. Managers can make sure that temporarily less-engaged
   employees still know what's going on in terms of policies or
   project changes, and can update them on changes in direction
   or focus. This suggestion is true both for employees who stay
   with the organization in reduced roles and also for those who
   leave. When the labor market is tight, many firms find that their
   best source of new recruits is their alumni.

5. *Find ways for alternaters to keep their skills sharp.* One risk for
   alternaters who scale back their work commitment is appearing

uninterested in developmental opportunities. Moreover, many professionals who scale back feel that they are expected to accomplish the same results in less time, which means that development time may be sacrificed for accomplishing their immediate objectives. Managers can be extremely helpful by both setting clear expectations for continuing development and by offering projects and work assignments that will keep people involved, even when they are spending fewer hours at work.

TIPS FOR MANAGING OUTSOURCERS

Although these suggestions are slanted toward managers, many are equally applicable to an outsourcer's coworkers. The benefits are obvious: If you can help people spend less time and energy worrying about important aspects of their nonwork lives, they will be more productive on the job and (potentially) more loyal to the work group and/or company.

1. *Make sure people are aware of on-site services.* It's surprising how many people don't realize that their employer offers on-site auto care, for example, or take-home meals from the cafeteria. Make it a point to communicate such benefits the moment a new employee joins your team. Get to know your people well enough that you can refer them to specific company-sponsored services that may help them make their lives less complicated.

2. *Help identify off-site resources.* For services not provided by your company, you can still play a key role in helping people outsource. Find out what services your direct reports and others are most interested in and then help them locate convenient, trustworthy, affordable, or otherwise desirable providers. It's easy to set up a referral network for childcare, for example. It doesn't cost anything, yet it can greatly simplify the process of

finding reliable options. The same goes for health clubs, house cleaning, yard care, local merchants, and other services. The collective experience of your employee base can be powerfully accessed via a services directory on your company's intranet, where employees can recommend providers, give ratings of their services, share warnings about poor service, and post help-wanted requests. If such a site doesn't now exist, create one.

3. *Coach people on delegation and planning techniques.* As a manager, you ought to be doing this anyway. Delegation and planning are important skills in any work setting, especially for developing future leadership talent. They're also core competencies for effective outsourcing. Cultivate the ability of your people to organize projects, plan for contingencies, set clear expectations, and hold others accountable. These are highly transferable skills that will help your employees be more effective on and off the job—the ultimate win/win situation.

4. *Be flexible.* When one of your staff needs to implement a back-up plan, be as accommodating as the situation allows. As a manager, you're constantly faced with variations on this theme: "My babysitting fell through this morning. Do I have to be at the staff meeting or can I call in from home?" Employees watch closely your reactions and decisions. It's a fool's errand to try to please everyone. Make sure your policies for dealing with such requests never compromise the business. But remember, the way you deal with others' needs for occasional flexibility will have a direct impact on their willingness to extend the same understanding when your sprinkler system malfunctions and begins flooding your basement.

Also, you need to know your staff members well enough to respect the times when they are particularly not available. For Chris Watson, this means Sundays; for Joel Klein, it's the family dinner hour (see chapter 4).

5. *Compensation is important.* Is compensation ever not important, you ask? The point here is that outsourcing can be expensive. If you have an especially talented employee who is
deserving of a raise, that may be the best step you can take to
help with his or her work-life balance.

TIPS FOR MANAGING BUNDLERS

If you're a manager or team leader, chances are that some of
your direct reports use this approach—or could use it more with
your help. The following guidelines could help them increase their
efficiency.

1. *Align work assignments with nonwork priorities.* "I've found that
something as simple as letting direct reports choose which conferences they want to attend makes a big difference, because
when they choose the conference, they choose the location,"
says Camille Harrells, introduced in chapter 5. "They might
combine the business trip with a family vacation, or a visit to
friends or relatives along the way. We also try to take personal
interests in mind when we're assigning projects in other states.
If we know that someone's parents live in a particular area, we
try to let them manage all of the projects in that area. In the
long run, it usually ends up saving us travel costs, and saves a
lot of wear and tear on our people."

Taking personal interests into consideration can also buy
increased employee loyalty. Denise Rich, a Toronto-based sales
executive, confirmed the benefits of this approach. "During a
biking vacation in New Zealand this spring, I met a guy that
I'm really crazy about. The only problem is he lives in Southern
California. A few weeks later, I got an e-mail from my boss
(who knew about the relationship) reminding me about some

training that I had agreed to complete before the end of the fiscal year. I hadn't attended the workshop because it was only held in other regions and I hadn't been very motivated to fit in the extra travel time. She pointed out that there was an upcoming session planned for our regional office in Los Angeles. 'Maybe you can save us some money by staying with friends,' she wrote in the note. That really meant a lot to me."

2. *Allow flexibility in completing assignments; let people set their own agendas.* In addition to matching travel destinations with personal interests, Kelly Baker (see chapter 5) noted that it's important for managers to let bundlers set their own agenda. "I've had managers who were skeptical about my ability to accomplish everything that I needed to in the amount of time available. In the worst cases, they started trying to micromanage me, requiring that I accomplish everything according to their plan, not mine. The most helpful managers are those who have trusted me to get things done, even if they couldn't see how I was going to do it."

Encouraging bundling can also produce great results for the organization. Kevin Childers (profiled in chapter 5) points out that his department was able to eliminate a number of meetings when they started to look for meeting redundance. Camille Harrells has taken a similar approach in planning new initiatives. "Our resources are usually quite scarce, so we have to choose carefully which projects to support. If we can find a way to do two projects for the price of one, we can accomplish twice as much." For example, the company she works for recently launched a team-building initiative and also wanted to explore redesigning the organization. Both activities required the use of cross-functional teams and a similar meeting format. By using the redesign project as a laboratory for building team skills, they accomplished both objectives in one year. With a different approach, one initiative would have been sacrificed.

3. *Provide schedule flexibility.* "My manager doesn't care when I work, as long as I get the job done," said Kevin Childers—a quote that could have been attributed to many of the bundlers we interviewed. It's easier to overcome boundaries when the artificial barriers of arbitrary schedule requirements are removed. Obviously, not every job allows for flextime. However, in far too many large organizations, "face time" during traditional office hours has outlived its usefulness as a performance criterion. "Our company has designated core hours when everyone needs to be in the office—a six-hour block in the middle of the day," says Gina Caldwell (see chapter 5). "My manager is great about letting me work around that time block, which allows me to balance my other priorities."

TIPS FOR MANAGING TECHFLEXERS

Telework demands a great deal of flexibility on the manager's end. Fortunately, most large companies that promote remote work in certain jobs also require training, provide guidelines, and offer customized reporting systems. Hewlett-Packard provides a tool for managers called Managing Remotely, for example, and quarterly Remote Management Forms to ease the process of keeping tabs on their dispersed workforce.

Whether or not your company is as enlightened as Hewlett-Packard, here are some basic pointers for maximizing the productivity and satisfaction of your would-be electronic cottage workers.

1. *Assess fit.* Chances are you see the employee's work with a bit more objectivity than he or she does. You need to be candid

about two issues. First, does the job lend itself to remote work? Second, does the employee fit the characteristics defined earlier in this chapter: self-starting, able to maintain long-distance relationships, low need for direct social interaction? You're not doing anyone a favor, no matter how urgent the apparent need, by setting him or her up for failure. In fact, many experts recommend ignoring the employee's personal situation entirely. "This is a business decision, and our policy is to make it reason-blind," says Carolyn Maddux, human resources vice president at Don Hunt's company (see chapter 6). "Employees come in with these very poignant stories about their personal needs, and we have to say, 'We understand and empathize, but that's not the point of this policy.' It's not that we don't care, we just can't require managers to judge if one person's personal issue is more valid than the next person's. Going back to grad school or caring for an aging parent—which is more important? That's why we're adamant that the only relevant consideration is, 'Will the job get done?'"

2. *Set clear, measurable expectations.* This point applies to all employees, of course. It is particularly helpful for techflexers, however, since the manager can't pop into their office for a quick redefinition of the assignment or offer an impromptu midcourse correction in the hallway. Strive for unambiguous descriptions of their role, and agree on what excellent performance looks like. The better you define the desired outcomes, the more likely the techflexer will be productive.

3. *Overcommunicate.* Managers should be in contact with their techflexers at least daily. Whether it's a simple e-mail, a more detailed project review, or a coaching conversation, make sure it happens. This kind of checking in may seem superfluous, but it's a vital antidote to the out-of-sight, out-of-mind problem.

4. *Provide access to technical support.* This almost goes without saying, but we mention it just in case.

5. *Encourage social interaction.* As a manager, you know that a techflexing employee is vulnerable by not being present at the office. Take measures to help the employee network and stay in the loop on office politics. You may want to encourage your people to attend certain meetings and events, come to the office periodically, interface with key members of the management team, and build a strong personal network. You can play a powerful role in keeping the techflexer connected.

6. *Represent and communicate the employee's value.* Again, this is solid advice for all of your staff. It just happens to be more urgent for techflexers. Since often they aren't around to market themselves and call attention to their brilliance and contributions, you can earn their undying loyalty if you're willing to do this for them. Their face may not be seen around the office, but their name should be well known for the work that they do. (All of this assumes, of course, that they're doing great work.)

TIPS FOR MANAGING SIMPLIFIERS

A growing percentage of professionals are embracing simplifying as their primary strategy for rebalancing. In some ways, this strategy runs against the key interests of most organizations, where long-term, intense commitment is preferred over a more guarded sense of loyalty. However, as the labor market continues to be tight, and as key contributors feel they've earned the right to set more aggressive boundaries between themselves and their jobs, many managers will find it in their best interest to accommodate a lesser devotion to the job or the organization. The following tips should help.

1. *Be clear about the individual's key strengths and talents.* One key to using simplifiers successfully is to zero in on the things that they do uniquely well or the unusual strengths they bring to the organization. By tapping those strengths, a manager can maximize a simplifier's contribution while also respecting her boundaries. Managers can also be aware of what capability they may lose if they pressure someone who doesn't fit the mold of working more intensively.

2. *Be clear about what the organization needs most from simplifiers.* Simplifiers can often make remarkable contributions to the organizations where they work. Managers can tap skills and talents by discussing goals and priorities often and clearly with simplifiers. "I made a lot of progress with my current manager when I initiated a discussion about where her needs and my strengths overlapped," one simplifier told us. Since many simplifiers may not be inclined to initiate such a discussion, managers can take the lead and clarify expectations.

3. *Recognize that it may be better to keep a top performer part time than to lose him full time.* As with alternating, simplifying will always raise concerns about an individual's ability to contribute. Can you trust someone who doesn't seem fully committed to manage relationships with key customers? Can someone really be an effective manager if he won't work overtime? Will it frustrate this person's internal clients if they aren't in the office to take phone calls all day, every day? A willingness to experiment and try flexible approaches, such as flextime or telecommuting, will often show that even if some concerns are warranted, the overall cost to the organization will be less by accommodating the simplifier than by losing him.

4. *Look for ways to keep simplifiers in the loop, even when they may not be physically in the office.* Managers can make sure that less engaged employees still know what's going on in terms of

policies or project changes and can update them on changes in direction or focus. While part of this is just a matter of kindness in helping simplifiers cope, it can also serve the manager's interests by maintaining the appropriate level of integration among members of the team or group.

5. *Find ways for simplifiers to keep their skills sharp.* One risk for simplifiers who have scaled back their work commitments while attempting to make the same contribution is appearing uninterested in developmental opportunities. Managers can be extremely helpful by both setting clear expectations for continuing development and by offering projects and work assignments that will keep people involved, even when they are spending fewer hours at work. This can also turn out to be a boon for managers, who will reap the benefits of having increased capability in their group over time.

NOTES

CHAPTER 1: A NEW HOLY GRAIL

1. "How Employers and Workers Can Strike the Balance," *Work Trends II: Work and Family,* March 1999, p. 1. The *Work Trends* survey is a joint project of the John J. Heldrich Center for Workforce Development at Rutgers University and the Center for Survey Research at the University of Connecticut. You can order a full report or download an executive summary by visiting the Heldrich Center's Web site: www.heldrich.rutgers.edu.

2. Ellen Galinsky and A. A. Johnson, *Reframing the Business Case for Work-Life Initiatives,* Pub. #W98-02 of the Families and Work Institute, 1998. This booklet is available by visiting the institute's Web site: www.familiesandwork.org.

3. A summary of our own research can be obtained by contacting us at our Web site: www.beyondjuggling.com.

4. Sue Shellenbarger, *Work and Family: Essays from the "Work and Family" Column of the Wall Street Journal* (New York: Ballantine Books, 1999).

5. Steven Greenhouse, "Americans' International Lead in Hours Worked Grew in 90's, Report Shows," *New York Times,* 1 September 2001, A8. According to the United Nations International Labor Organization, the United States earned the distinction of the "hardest working" industrialized nation starting in 1999 and widened its lead in 2000 (the latest year for which statistics were available at the time of this writing). U.S. workers used to labor about the same number of hours as their European counterparts. But over the past two decades, European workers' average hours have been declining as ours have been increasing.

6. Anna Muoio, "Balancing Acts," *Fast Company* (February/March 1999): 84–88.

CHAPTER 2: A NATION OF JUGGLERS

1. *101 Facts on the Status of Women* (Washington, D.C.: Business and Professional Women's Foundation, 2000), 1.
2. Shellenbarger, *Work and Family,* 45.
3. Richard W. Judy and Carol D'Amico, *Workforce 2020: Work and Workers* (Indianapolis: Hudson Institute, 1999), 91.
4. The measure for working mothers with children under age six is from Maureen Milford, "Ozzie at the Office; Harriet at Home," *Salt Lake Tribune,* 13 November 1995, B1, B6. The reference concerning working mothers with children of all ages is from *101 Facts.*
5. *101 Facts.*
6. Alice Lesch Kelly, "For Employed Moms, the Pinnacle of Stress Comes after Work Ends," *New York Times,* 13 June 1999, sec. 15, p. 18. The percentages of household chores performed by men versus women are from research by Dr. Rosalind Barnett of the Women's Studies Program at Brandeis University.
7. Peter Cappelli, *The New Deal at Work: Managing the Market-Driving Workforce* (Boston: Harvard Business School Press, 1999). Cappelli provides data and insight from the huge layoffs and downsizing of the early 1990s. Employee motivation and productivity, he says, are as dependent on labor market demand as they are on leadership and corporate culture. Without other viable choices, employees are willing to suffer low morale, burn-out, and job dissatisfaction—and still behave productively. If, instead, they have numerous job choices, they may leave even a well-paying job for more job-related benefits, such as work-life programs, greater flexibility, and/or better training and development opportunities.
8. Robert B. Reich, *The Future of Success* (New York: Alfred A. Knopf, 2001) 7–8. The former labor secretary's penetrating analysis of life in the new economy has had a profound influence on our thinking.
9. Despite the laments of traditionalists that women are working simply to maintain luxurious lifestyles, the picture of family finances tells a different story. While the median family income is about $48,000 a year, families with a single wage-earner average only $21,000. Dual-career couples, in contrast, earned an average of $61,000 in 1998. (Cited in Larry Williams and Mary Otto, "Sense of Unease for U.S. Workers," *Salt Lake Tribune,* 6 September 1999, A1, A8.) Thus, that second paycheck makes a significant difference. One in three adults report that they don't have enough income to make ends meet. They live with the stress of constant—sometimes acute—scarcity. (Source: Molly Ivins, "In the Hourglass Economy, Working Majority Needs to be Heard." *Salt Lake Tribune,* 6 September 1999, A13.)

    In addition, the cost of big-ticket items has risen sharply in the past 20 years. For instance, in constant-dollar terms, the cost of education at a public college has climbed by 37%, new housing by 31%, a new car by 66%, education at a private college by 67%, and day care by 202%. (See Betsy Morris, "Is Your Family Wrecking Your Career?" *Fortune* (17 March 1997): 71–82.) The sharp rise in day care prices particularly highlights the working family's plight. As more mothers join the workforce, the demand for good day care increases, pushing up the cost. A working mother (and her partner, if she has one) has to work even harder to keep the children in day care. But even with the growing cost of day care, many mothers and fathers still find it necessary for their overall finances to work outside the home.

10. This discussion owes a great debt to the work of Edgar Schein. He first proposed the idea of the internal and external careers in 1971. (See Edgar H. Schein, "The Individual, the Organization and the Career: A Conceptual Scheme," *Journal of Applied Behavioral Science* 7 (1971): 401–426). Schein went on to study and label internal career "anchors," connoting the idea that we are attached to this identity regardless of the ups and downs of our "external" careers (job changes, layoffs, reorganizations, promotions, etc.). Anchors are basic values and motives that individuals do not relinquish. (See Edgar H. Schein, *Career Dynamics* [Reading, Mass.: Addison-Wesley, 1978]).

Douglas Hall built on this work with his theory of the "protean career," named after the Greek god Proteus, who knew how to reinvent himself after being destroyed by external forces. Hall maintains that knowing one's career self in the fast-changing new economy is the only long-term stability. (See Douglas T. Hall, "Protean Careers of the 21st Century," *The Academy of Management Executive* x, no. 4 (November 1996): 8–16.

Finally, one of this book's authors (Brooklyn Derr) has dedicated much of his adult life to exploring the intricacies of the internal career. Expanding on Schein's work, Derr describes five dominant "career orientations" that tend to remain stable over the course of a person's life, though they can change due to external forces. (See C. Brooklyn Derr, *Managing the New Careerists: The Diverse Career Success Orientations of Today's Workers* [San Francisco: Jossey-Bass, 1986], and C. Brooklyn Derr and A. Laurent, "The Internal and External Career: A Theoretical and Cross-Cultural Perspective" in *Handbook of Career Theory*, ed. M. B. Arthur, B. Laurence, and D. T. Gall [New York: Cambridge University Press, 1989], 454–471.)

11. Tongue-in-cheek but nonetheless compelling, Akst's call to arms appeared in his column entitled "Workaholics Arise. Now Get Back to Work," *New York Times,* 6 May 2001, sec. 3, p. 3.

12. Reich chronicles society's trend away from marriage and children in a chapter entitled "The Incredible Shrinking Family," in *The Future of Success*. Robert D. Putnam argues forcefully that a variety of factors (longer work hours among them) has resulted in less community involvement and dwindling participation in church and non-work-related social activities. The title of his book is evocative: *Bowling Alone: The Collapse and Revival of American Community* (New York: Simon and Schuster, 2000).

13. Sue Shellenbarger, "One Couple Has Mastered the Art of a Balanced Life," *Wall Street Journal,* 16 May 2001.

14. This estimate of membership in the voluntary simplicity movement comes from an article in *U.S. News & World Report* ("Doing Well, Not Doing Without," 14 December 1998, p. 60). As for our belief that simplifying will never be the dominant work-life balance strategy, Reich makes a strong case: "If you think that cutting your costs of living will simplify your life, think again. Deciding on your 'needs' doesn't avoid the difficulty of making a hard choice, because the choice isn't really between paid work and the rest of your life. It's between one kind of busy-ness and another. . . . If you want to free up more time and energy for the rest of your life by working and earning less, then some of the things that now make the rest of your life easier or more pleasurable will have to be jettisoned, because you won't be able to afford them" (*The Future of Success,* 231).

15. Muoio, "Balancing Acts."

16. Susan Miller, "The Role of the Juggler," in *Integrating Work and Family,* ed. Saroj Parasuraman and Jeffrey H. Greenhaus (Westport, Conn.: Quorum Books, 1997), 48–56.

17. Dyson's address was delivered at Georgia Tech's 172nd commencement on September 6, 1991. A copy of the full text is available by contacting Dyson's office at the Coca-Cola Company in Atlanta, Georgia. An excerpt containing the passage about juggling can be found at www.princeton.edu/~tktan/life.html (as of January 2002).

CHAPTER 3: ALTERNATING

1. Felice N. Schwartz, "Management Women and the New Facts of Life," *Harvard Business Review* (January/February 1989).

CHAPTER 4: OUTSOURCING

1. "How Much Is Enough?" *Fast Company* 26 (July/August 1999): 108–112.

2. "Outsource Your Life," *Fortune Small Business* (December/January 2000): 101–102.

3. Arlie Hochschild, "Broadening the Horizons: The Thick and Thin of Care," (paper presented at Work and Family: Expanding the Horizons Conference, San Francisco, Calif., 3 March 2000).

4. Barbara A. Gutek, "Services and Work-Family Life" in *Integrating Work and Family,* ed. Saroj Parasuraman and Jeffrey H. Greenhaus (Westport, Conn.: Quorum Books, 1997), 77–90.

5. Ibid.

6. DeGroot is quoted in Shellenbarger, *Work and Family,* 106.

CHAPTER 5: BUNDLING

1. Marc Gunther, "Faith and Fortune," *Fortune* (9 July 2001).
2. Ibid.
3. Lyle Hanna's story is recounted in Brian O'Keefe and Theodore Spencer, "Making Time for Not Making Money," *Fortune* (18 December 2000).

CHAPTER 6: TECHFLEXING

1. Todd Lappin, "When the Cubicle Has a Crankshaft," *New York Times,* 14 June 2001, G1.
2. Linda Saslow, "Telecommuting: Bye, L.I.R.R., Ciao, L.I.E." *New York Times,* 12 September 1999, sec. 14LI, p. 1.
3. These statistics are from a Conference Board study, cited by Maggie Jackson in "Work Finds Its Way Home in the 90's," *Salt Lake Tribune,* 5 August 1999, E1, E5.
4. Francine Riley and Donna Weaver McClosky, "Telecommuting as a Response to Help People Balancing Work and Family," in *Integrating Work and Family,* ed. Saroj Parasuraman and Jeffrey H. Greenhaus (Westport, Conn.: Quorum Books, 1977), 133–142.
5. "How Much Is Enough?"
6. Sue Shellenbarger, "These Telecommuters Just Barely Maintain Their Office Decorum," *Wall Street Journal,* 24 September 1997, B1.
7. E. Jeffrey Hill, "IBM Worldwide Survey," unpublished data, Brigham Young University, Family Studies Center, 1054 SWKT, Provo, UT 84602, 1998.
8. "Groceries to Go," *Kiplinger's* (August 2001): 97–98.
9. E. Jeffrey Hill, A. J. Hawkins, and M. Weitzman, "Finding an Extra Day a Week: The Positive Effect of Job Flexibility on Work and Family Life Balance." *Family Relations* 50, no. 1: 49–58.
10. E. Jeffrey Hill, Brent C. Miller, Sara P. Weiner, and Joe Colihan, "Influences of the Virtual Office on Aspects of Work and Work/Life Balance," *Personnel Psychology* 51 (1998): 667–683.
11. Reed Abelson, "A Push from the Top Shatters a Glass Ceiling," *New York Times,* 22 August 1999, sec. 1, p. 1.
12. Keith H. Hammonds and Gabrielle Saveri, "Can Ernst and Young Retain Women by Rethinking Work?" *Business Week* (23 February 1998).
13. Shellenbarger, *Work and Family,* 209.

CHAPTER 7: SIMPLIFYING

1. John DeGraff, Davin Wann, and Thomas H. Naylor, *Affluenza: The All-Consuming Epidemic* (San Francisco: Berrett-Koehler, 2001), 24.

2. Ibid., 14.
3. Ibid., 21.
4. Ibid.
5. Ibid.
6. Ibid., 6.
7. Michael Warshaw, "Keep It Simple," *Fast Company* 15 (June/July 1998): 154.
8. Ibid.
9. Michael Kidd, "White Paper on Self-Storage" Self-Storage Association (March 2000).
10. Putnam, *Bowling Alone*.

CHAPTER 8: QUESTION YOUR ASSUMPTIONS

1. Greenhouse, "Americans' International Lead in Hours Worked Grew in 90's."
2. Dhitiporn Chompookum, "Career Orientations and Organizational Citizenship Behavior in Thailand" (Ph.D. diss. David Eccles School of Business, University of Utah, August 2001).
3. The Venezuelan study was reported in a paper delivered at the International Congress of Applied Psychology on August 10, 1998. (Elena Granell de Alaz and Claudia Malpica, "360 Degree Feedback as a Management Tool in a Business School," unpublished paper, available from Elena Granell de Alaz, Center for Human Development and Organizations, Institute for Advanced Studies in Administration, Ave. IESE, Edif. IESE, San Bernadino, Apdo. 1640, Caracas 1010A, Venezuela.) For more information on Brooklyn Derr's Career Success Map self-assessment or to take the assessment on-line, please visit www.beyondjuggling.com.
4. Robert Taylor, "Longer Holidays Make More Sense," *Financial Times*, 15 June 2001, p. viii.
5. Edgar H. Schein, *Organizational Culture and Leadership* (San Francisco: Jossey-Bass, 1985).

CHAPTER 9: ASSESS YOUR IMBALANCE

1. The Balance Strategies Profile (BSP) and the strategies featured in it were originally derived from approximately 125 interviews with professionals across a variety of industries and professional roles. We created an original assessment, which was tested with a variety of working professionals from across the United States, as well as with a class of executive MBA students at the University of Utah. During this testing, we discovered that some of the strategies we had identified weren't being used by anyone, which led us to revise the categories and the items. We also found some overlap between the strategies,

which we resolved. The profile was then tested again with more than 500 professionals across the United States and Europe. The BSP featured here is a result of that testing, augmented by continuing interviews to gain additional insight into the strategies.

2. Daniel J. Levinson, et al., *The Seasons of a Man's Life* (New York: Alfred A. Knopf, 1978); Daniel J. Levinson with Judy D. Levinson, *The Seasons of a Woman's Life* (New York: Random House, 1997); and Gail Sheehy, *Passages: Predictable Crises of Adult Life* (New York: Bantam Doubleday Dell, 1997).

3. Muoio, "Balancing Acts," 86.

CHAPTER 10: REBALANCE YOUR LIFE

1. The Career Orientations model is described in detail in C. Brooklyn Derr, *Managing the New Careerists* (San Francisco: Jossey-Bass, 1986). Copies of the Career Success Map, an instrument that helps individuals assess their internal career values, are available from the authors at www.beyondjuggling.com.

APPENDIX

1. Dave Ulrich, "Intellectual Capital = Competence × Commitment," *Sloan Management Review* 39, no. 2 (winter 1998): 15–26.

2. Albert O. Hirschman, *Exit, Voice, and Loyalty: Responses to Decline in Firms, Organizations, and States* (Cambridge, Mass.: Harvard University Press, 1972).

INDEX

ABOUT THE AUTHORS

KURT W. SANDHOLTZ

Kurt Sandholtz is a writer, speaker, and career development consultant. For twelve years, Sandholtz led the career development practice at BT.Novations, a respected human resources consulting firm, where he worked with corporations such as Intel, DuPont, General Mills, Fidelity Investments, Dell, and Procter & Gamble. He spent the early part of his career as a staff writer and editor for the *Wall Street Journal's National Business Employment Weekly*.

Work-life balance is a constant battle for Sandholtz. While he loves his work, he's equally passionate about his family. Together they enjoy camping, hiking, skiing, and playing music. Inspired by the people he interviewed for *Beyond Juggling*, he negotiated a four-day work week and took a commensurate voluntary pay cut in order to have the time he needed to write this book and keep up with his other priorities, which include church service, cooking, and coaching soccer. A reformed juggler, he is now trying to alternate and outsource.

C. BROOKLYN DERR, ED.D.

Brooklyn Derr is a world-renowned expert on managing people in the new global economy. A professor of management at the Marriott School of Management, Brigham Young University (BYU), Derr is also a permanent visiting professor at the Lyon Graduate School of Management (EM Lyon) in France. Over the past fifteen years, Derr has traveled the world researching and discussing topics such as career dynamics, managing high-potentials, leadership development, internationalizing future leaders, and why work-life issues are critical in recruiting, retaining, and motivating talent.

Derr is well regarded for his theory of career orientations (five ways talented people define career-life success). In some ways, *Beyond Juggling* is a sequel to his earlier book, *Managing the New Careerists* (Jossey-Bass, 1986). He is one of the founders of the Careers Division of the American Academy of Management. Derr is the author of six books and over forty scholarly articles and book chapters. His most recent book, *Cross-Cultural Leadership Development,* was published by Quorum Books in 2002.

Derr has taught executives at companies such as Warner Lambert, Texas Instruments, Johnson & Johnson, Kodak, Zurich Insurance, and Groupe Total. He has also taught executives and MBAs at BYU; the University of Utah; EM Lyon; the International Management Institute (IMD) in Lausanne, Switzerland; the European Institute of Business Administration (INSEAD) in Fontainebleau, France; Chualalongkorn University in Bangkok, Thailand; and Doung-Hua University in Shanghai, China.

At home in Alpine, Utah, Derr derives pleasure from working in his large vegetable garden and riding his Morgan horse in the nearby Rocky Mountains. (His balance strategy is split between juggling and alternating.) He is active in his church, is a board member of the Alpine Sculpture Park Foundation, and is president of the Harvard Alumni Association of Utah. His wife, Jill, is a historian at BYU, and together they try to keep tabs on four active adult children and one grandson. To change scenery and add variety to their country life, the Derrs live each October–November in an apartment near Place de Sathonay in Lyon, France's second largest city. Derr teaches at EM Lyon, Jill writes, and together they explore Lyon's museums and fine restaurants, go to concerts and the theater, and visit the surrounding rural countryside.

KATHY BUCKNER

Kathy Buckner is vice president of consulting services for BT.Novations and a nationally known expert in career and employee development. She has led global career initiatives in organizations such as General Electric, Ford Motor Company, DuPont, General Mills, K-mart, Philips, and Estee Lauder. Buckner has worked successfully with professionals and their leaders in a variety of industries, countries, and professional disciplines. Her professional passion is helping both individuals and organizations to realize their potential. She has spoken at national and regional conferences and authored numerous articles and book chapters on a variety of career-related topics.

After completing a master's degree in organizational behavior at Brigham Young University, Buckner was director of the Utah Small Business Development Center, where she managed training and management development services for a wide range of entrepreneurs, from mom-and-pop retailers to emerging high-tech firms. Before joining BT.Novations, she owned her own consulting firm.

In her time away from work, Buckner's primary interests include international adventure travel, snow skiing, backpacking, mountain biking, reading, and playing the organ at church. She's an alternater with strong simplifying tendencies and is working hard at learning how to bundle.

DAWN S. CARLSON, PH.D.

Dawn Carlson is an assistant professor of management at the Hankamer School of Business, Baylor University. Carlson has had a longstanding interest in the area of work-life balance and has built a strong reputation in the field. Her doctoral research on work-family conflict won the 1995 Women in Management "best dissertation" award from the Academy of Management. Carlson has published a number of research papers on this topic, including work exploring coping behaviors, mentoring, measuring work-family conflict, career development, personality, and social support.

Carlson's expertise in questionnaire design and validation has been crucial to *Beyond Juggling*. She led the development of the Balance Strategies Profile (BSP). In addition to being a valid and reliable measure of work-life balance strategies, the BSP is also an easy-to-use and diagnostically helpful tool. As part of the creation of the BSP, Carlson managed the testing and retesting of the tool with groups of volunteers to refine both its psychometric and usability characteristics.

Carlson is a popular teacher and an engaging speaker. She has presented work-life research at national and international conferences. In addition, her passion for balance goes well beyond her scholarly interests: Carlson is married and has three young children (a toddler and eight-month-old twins). She and her husband, John (also a professor at Baylor), have chosen careers that allow them some scheduling flexibility. The balance strategies that the Carlsons use most are juggling and techflexing. They both enjoy working in the garden, traveling, snow skiing, and reading— although, at the moment, their main focus is on their children and the associated diapers and messes.

To contact the authors for information about seminars, workshops, speeches, or assessments, please visit their Web site: www. beyondjuggling.com.

Berrett-Koehler Publishers

B ERRETT-KOEHLER is an independent publisher of books, periodicals, and other publications at the leading edge of new thinking and innovative practice on work, business, management, leadership, stewardship, career development, human resources, entrepreneurship, and global sustainability.

Since the company's founding in 1992, we have been committed to supporting the movement toward a more enlightened world of work by publishing books, periodicals, and other publications that help us to integrate our values with our work and work lives, and to create more humane and effective organizations.

We have chosen to focus on the areas of work, business, and organizations, because these are central elements in many people's lives today. Furthermore, the work world is going through tumultuous changes, from the decline of job security to the rise of new structures for organizing people and work. We believe that change is needed at all levels—individual, organizational, community, and global—and our publications address each of these levels.

We seek to create new lenses for understanding organizations, to legitimize topics that people care deeply about but that current business orthodoxy censors or considers secondary to bottom-line concerns, and to uncover new meaning, means, and ends for our work and work lives.

See next page for other publications
from Berrett-Koehler

Whistle While You Work
Heeding Your Life's Calling

Richard J. Leider and David A. Shapiro

We all have have a calling in life. It needs only to be uncovered, not discovered. *Whistle While You Work* makes the uncovering process inspiring and fun. Featuring a unique "Calling Card" exercise—a powerful way to put the whistle in your work—it is a liberating and practical guide that will help you find work that is truly satisfying, deeply fulfilling, and consistent with your deepest values.

Paperback original, 200 pages • ISBN 1-57675-103-1
Item #51031-407 $15.95

Repacking Your Bags
Lighten Your Load for the Rest of Your Life
Second Edition

Richard J. Leider and David A. Shapiro

Learn how to climb out from under the many burdens you're carrying and find the fulfillment that's missing in your life. A simple yet elegant process teaches you to balance the demands of work, love, and place in order to create and live your own vision of success.

Paperback, 260 pages • ISBN 1-57675-180-5 • Item #51805-407 $16.95

The Power of Purpose
Creating Meaning in Your Life and Work

Richard J. Leider

We all possess a unique ability to do the work we were made for. Concise and easy to read, and including numerous stories of people living on purpose, *The Power of Purpose* is a remarkable tool to help you find your calling, an original guide to discovering the work you love to do.

Hardcover, 170 pages • ISBN 1-57675-021-3 • Item #50213-407 $20.00
Audio, 2 cassettes • ISBN 1-57453-215-4 • Item #32154-407 $17.95

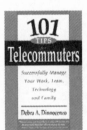